KALEIDOSCOPE

DERBYSHIRE

Edited by Michelle Warrington

First published in Great Britain in 1999 by
POETRY NOW YOUNG WRITERS
Remus House,
Coltsfoot Drive,
Woodston,
Peterborough, PE2 9JX
Telephone (01733) 890066

HB ISBN 0 75430 662 3
SB ISBN 0 75430 663 1

FOREWORD

This year, the Poetry Now Young Writers' Kaleidoscope competition proudly presents the best poetic contributions from over 32,000 up-and-coming writers nationwide.

Successful in continuing our aim of promoting writing and creativity in children, each regional anthology displays the inventive and original writing talents of 11-18 year old poets. Imaginative, thoughtful, often humorous, *Kaleidoscope Derbyshire* provides a captivating insight into the issues and opinions important to today's young generation.

The task of editing inevitably proved challenging, but was nevertheless enjoyable thanks to the quality of entries received. The thought, effort and hard work put into each poem impressed and inspired us all. We hope you are as pleased as we are with the final result and that you continue to enjoy *Kaleidoscope Derbyshire* for years to come.

CONTENTS

Ben Eveson	38
Adam Whatton	38
Nicola Jane Wyldbore	39
Emma Stones	40
Vicki Gibson	40
Katie Rogers	41
Stacey Smalley	42
Nicholas Walters	42
Lauren England	43
Adam Reville	43
Megan L Walters	44
Laura Bednarz	45
Rachel Rawson	45
Melissa Shields	46
Jamie Bunting	46
Carla Ryntowt	47
Kayleigh Blythe	47
Tara Graney	48
Nicole Atkinson	48
Robert Cairns	49
Kirsty Atherton	49
Liz Smith	50

Highfields School

Alice Jane Milner	51
Charlotte Fletcher	51
Edmund Hunt	52
Danielle Crawford	53
Grant Baynes	54
Amy Oldershaw	54
Naomi Smallman	55
Rupert Hoskin	56
Chris Roberts	56
Sarah Whittington	57
Adam Varkalis	57
Sam Blood	58

James White	58
Steve Hicklin	59
James Wardman	59
Claire Drinkall	60
Becki Burrell	60
Adam Ward	61
Bryony Stevens	61
Daniel Johnson	62
David Hayward	63
Christy Britland	63
Lucy Brameld	64
Lyndsay Broome	64
James McElvaney	65
Holly Kirkland	65
Charlotte Liddicot	66
Jennifer Arran	66
Jessica Inglis	67
Michael Williamson	68
Melanie Keep	68
Kate Smith	69
Adrienne Wood	69
Aaron Brough	70
Layla Fern	70
Matthew Statham	71
Laura Sandner	72
Gemma Fozzard	72
Elizabeth Tunna	73
Nicola Robinson	73
James Pearson	74
Paul Chapman	74
Melanie Smith	75
Victoria Marchant	75
Natalie Shooter	76
Cheryl Ward	76
Chlöe Newton	77
James Bance	78

Cliff Fawcett	78
Laura Donaldson	79
Ashley Statham	80
Nicola Lloyd	80
James Micallef	81
Matthew Cannon	82
Karl Newton	83
Chris Hardy	84
Sarah Hatch	85
Jamie Wood	85
Gregg Swift	86
Rachel Siddall	86
Abby Hampson	87
Nicola Morley	88
Sean Martin	89
Dean Kirkman	89
Erin Cooper	90
Gemma Smedley	90
Megan Pyne	91
William Wragg	92
Jessica Heaton	92
Chris Elliott	93
Kathryn Mann	93
Daniel Marchington	94
Laura Dowsett	94
William Matthew Young	95
Alice Vale	95
Karis Hodgkinson	96
Tom Wright	96
Adam Taylor	97
Lucie Needham	98
Alex Barker	98
Tom Harvey	99
Kirsten Hill	99
Suzanne Lilley	100
Cameron Freestone	100

John Flamsteed Community School

Carrieann White	164
Andy Kelly	164
Chris Briggs	165
Michelle Harrison	166
Haley Siddall	166
Laura McNeice	167
Barbara McNeice	167
Samantha Plater	168
Gareth Spolding	168
Jennifer Motley	169

St Thomas More School, Buxton

Christina McKechnie	169
Sara Kamali	170
Katie Shaw	170
Melanie Lath	171
Kathryn McKechnie	172
Ruth King	173
Genevieve Moore	173
Catherine Hurst	174
Helen Barber	174
Chantelle Salt	175
Matthew Scarbrough	176
Laura Martin	176
Caroline Wood	177
Katie Orridge	178
Olivia Lawton	179
Jay Fisher	180
Jennifer Thomson	181
Philip Hardman	182
David Della Cioppa	183
Vanessa Highet	184
Sergei Sellers	185
Bethan Youd	185
Fiona Edgar	186
Ellie Butterworth	187

The Poems

THE SNAKE

The snake it slithers on the ground,
It is trying to hide from the nasty hound,
It slithers here, it slithers there,
It is slithering everywhere.

He slithers all over the garden,
He doesn't even pardon,
He doesn't like it there,
He slithers away in despair.

He is as slippery as an eel;
But not as round as a wheel,
He doesn't make a sound,
As he slithers on the ground.

Ian Hilditch (11)
Chapel-en-le-Frith High School

THE HEDGEHOG

A brown little figure that scurries around,
Alone in the dark he makes no sound,
They are never in triplets nor even paired,
But if a predator comes they roll up in a ball
because they're scared.
Their spikes are like a conker in its shell,
But this conker does not shrivel up or swell,
When Christmas has come and children are merry,
And out comes the robin and the new berry.
The spiky, hungry, hasty hedgehog goes to sleep
till he hears the new born birds which sing 'Tweet tweet'.

Amy Large (11)
Chapel-en-le-Frith High School

THE BLACK CAT

As dark as the night
the black cat still comes in sight
around the haunted house

> As the witch on her broom
> comes down from the moon
> the cat spots a mouse

The mouse sees the cat
so he hides under the mat
the cat caught the mouse
under the house

> The witch caught the load
> and turned them into toads.

Helen Wilson (11)
Chapel-en-le-Frith High School

HEDGEHOG

H e waddles through the hedges,
E ver so slowly, as slowly as a tortoise,
D odging all the dangers by,
G racefully rolling into a ball,
E ventually he sleeps,
H ibernating through the winter,
O n he sleeps until the
G reenery grows and the sun is golden.

Lizi Norman (11)
Chapel-en-le-Frith High School

THE BAT

He flies so swiftly through the dark,
Its prey is sleeping so he's in luck,
It's night, no fear, nothing's near.

It's like a bullet so smooth and quick,
Gliding up and down, it hears a sound,
It finds its prey and then 'crunch'!

John Goodwin (11)
Chapel-en-le-Frith High School

THE CAT

This sneaky little animal
That prowls around at night
Crawling, climbing fences and creeping quietly
Looking for prey to catch at night
Then he sees his prey
And like a thunderbolt the prey is gone.

Adam Chesney (12)
Chapel-en-le-Frith High School

THE SNAKE

The snake slithers and slides
The snake hisses when prey is about
The snake is leathery and tough
The snake's colours are bright or dull.

Stephen Ashton (11)
Chapel-en-le-Frith High School

THE FOX

The sly and cunning fox creeps around,
Without making one single sound,
Its bushy tail swings from side to side,
Its eyes light up like a fairground ride.

At night he sneaks along the road,
And he hunts for his food without even being shown,
He hears the slightest little noise,
Then his ears shoot up like some little toys.

The dark, dingy darkness falls,
The sly cunning fox crawls.

Diane Thurston (11)
Chapel-en-le-Frith High School

THE LIZARD

The lizard sits upon a rock to cool down
As he sits upon the rock, he looks round non-stop
He sticks his tongue out and in, out and in
But he never gets tongue ache
He's always dashing hungrily about, looking for creepy crawlies
At the end of the night he doesn't manage to have a snack
At night he shuts his eyes and sleeps making noises
Click, click, click, click.

Thomas Baxter (11)
Chapel-en-le-Frith High School

THE BAT

The bat hangs up side down,
It fools around like a clown,
It hangs upside down,
All day long,
It sleeps all through the day,
And comes swooping all around the black, dark sky.

The bat sleeps in the day,
It does everything in its own way,
The bat likes to swoop around,
But not very much on the ground,
The bat wakes in the night.

Samantha Timpson (11)
Chapel-en-le-Frith High School

THE CAT

It creeps along the corridor, here and there,
Then it goes outside waiting silently for his prey,
Then he creeps slowly and pounces!
He has caught his prey,
Slowly he tears away, eating.
Then he walks away leaving it there to stay,
Then he goes back inside and curls up
In front of the fire and goes to sleep.

Katrina Sumner (11)
Chapel-en-le-Frith High School

TILLY

My cat is called Tilly,
She acts so very silly,
All she does is eat and play,
Through every hour in the day,
Her colour is as black as coal,
She purrs and puffs and pulls the pouffe.

She'll bite you if you annoy her,
She likes my dad most of all,
She likes playing with a ball,
She likes moping all around the living room floor,
Her favourite place is in front of the fire,
Her owners are me and my family.

Tara Birchenough (11)
Chapel-en-le-Frith High School

MY DOG BESS

My dog Bess is black;
With a strange ridge of hair on her back,
All she wants to do is play,
But she never will do what you say,
And after she's eaten her tea,
She decides she's picked up a flea,
She's scratching all night,
Then she wants to play fight,
And ends up giving *you* fleas!

Benjamin Stafford (11)
Chapel-en-le-Frith High School

THE CAT

He moves silently towards his prey,
One step, two steps, closer he gets,
Three steps, four steps, I have got you now!

Black and white, he moves closer to me,
Creeping, creeping he rubs against my leg,
He's trying to tell me, he's still hungry.

As I stroke him he purrs,
As he jumps on me he starts miaowing,
Silence falls, he's asleep now.

Rachel Harris (11)
Chapel-en-le-Frith High School

THE MONKEY

When the sun is out,
And the moon is down,
This animal swings from branches,
Hardly making a sound.
His fingers fumble for his far off favourite fruits,
In bunches of sevens to eights.

This creature moves slowly, steadily
In the hot day.
But when the winter nights draw near,
This animal need not hibernate.

Lerryn Brothers (11)
Chapel-en-le-Frith High School

THE SQUIRREL

A squirrel is a smallish creature
It has a lot of funny features
It's as active as another creature.

The squirrel jumps from tree to tree
As happy as can be.

It comes out at night
But we give it a fright.

Its prey is nuts and berries from up in the trees
It has to go up it, but not too high it goes
Then it goes to bed at night in the high, high trees.

Emily Cumbes (11)
Chapel-en-le-Frith High School

THE WANDERER

At least once a year a cat I know,
Wanders off in the summer holiday for around four weeks,
He had his owners in a mess,
But he doesn't care less.

He is like a runaway train but he walks and walks on,
He hunts like a lion prowls and stalks,
He is like that saying 'curiosity killed the cat',
He is very nosy, sometimes his nosiness is bad
And gets him into trouble.

John Everill (11)
Chapel-en-le-Frith High School

MY CAT ELLIE

My cat Ellie is as light as a feather
and as gentle as a dove
Yet when it comes to feeding time
she rushes to the kitchen as fast as lightning.

When I go to bed she slinks upstairs
as silent as a snake and settles down on my bed
and purrs softly putting me to sleep.

James Somerset (11)
Chapel-en-le-Frith High School

THE CAT

This sneaky cat crawls around at night,
Looking for something for supper tonight.
He sees his prey, watches,
The mouse is gone as quick as a flash.
Then he goes back to feed his litter,
On the way he is suspicious so he creeps carefully back.

Andrew Bell (11)
Chapel-en-le-Frith High School

THE CAT

It is quiet when the cat goes out,
you never hear a whisper,
the wind whirling wildly,
it's almost like a ghost town
with a black cat in the dark,
it's like hell, but in the day it's like heaven.

Chris Garlick (11)
Chapel-en-le-Frith High School

MY HAMSTER

I have a little hamster
Jasper is his name
He really is quite friendly
and very, very tame.

His fur is golden brown
his eyes are very bright
He likes to sleep throughout the day
and he likes to play at night.

I have to feed and play with him
and keep him nice and clean
He really is the nicest hamster
anyone has ever seen.

Lee Skelton (11)
Frederick Gent School

WHAT'S IN THE BOX?

In the box there might be a pair of smelly socks for me.
A couple of twins just to be as smelly as they can be.
Where did they come from?
I don't care.
Who do they belong to?
I don't know. How did they get here?
I don't really know, don't know.
Maybe from a footballer, maybe Paul Ince.

Alison Hand (11)
Frederick Gent School

ISLAND OF VOLCANOES

Hot air hits me as I step off the plane,
Step on the airport transport and ride into
a new country,
Realising I won't need my thick woolly
jumpers,
Exploring a new place,
Palms everywhere, clear green sea,
Sand dunes reach skywards in a gentle
curve,
Like a landscape of mountains, still and
forbidding,
Pitch black volcanoes reach for the sky,
Never knowing when to erupt,
Hot sun burning down, scorching everything
in its path,
A tropical, volcanic paradise,
Lanzarote.

Laura Jones (13)
Frederick Gent School

PARROT PALS

He sits there in his cage
Boring, boring, boring
All he keeps on doing is
Squawking, squawking, squawking.

He is green, yellow and orange
And about 18cm high
He eats chips, bread and pizza
And drinks beer and wine.

Daniel Hill (11)
Frederick Gent School

BEFORE AND AFTER MY PHOTO

I am four foot two
My eyes are blue
I hadn't a clue
For what I'd to do
So I sat and waited
With a cheesy grin
I stared into the camera
Flash!

It was all over
I walked from my seat
With my size one feet
I went in the classroom
Everyone was full of gloom
Then the week after
Screams of laughter
As they came
We all felt shame
But it was all right
And after all that fright
The pictures were fine.

Leah Crawford (11)
Frederick Gent School

THE DIVER

The diver dives deeply, secretly
Searching for sea shells while cold,
Wet fish are swimming in the sea,
While breathing bubbles float to the surface,
Where all the boats are floating around.

Craig Castledine (11)
Frederick Gent School

BUT 'JUNK-TION' 28

Junction 28, it surely lives up to its name,
The junk you see as you whiz around the island leaves
South Normanton in shame,
Crisp packets and crumpled chocolate wrappers and drinks cans too,
But we live here and we love it all the same.

I've been alive since '86 and it's steadily got worse,
Sometimes the cars go around the island as slow as a horse,
The fumes that come out of the cars surely damage our health,
But we live here and we love it all the same.

Junction 28, it surely lives up to its name,
The junk you see as you whiz around the island leaves
South Normanton in shame,
But we live here and we love it all the same,
It leaves South Normanton in shame,
But we live here and we love it all the same.

Samuel Neal (12)
Frederick Gent School

THE POODLE

A tail like a chimney sweep's brush
Black like he's rolled in coal
A tongue like a giant snake
Legs like they have been chopped off
Feet like ducks' flat feet
Teeth like jaws
Where? Where? He did not care
He rolls in the sand.

Shane Ford (11)
Frederick Gent School

A Lad Called?

He stood at his gate
With a gang of his mates
But I just stood there and stared.
A cute little boy with a handsome face
With blue gleaming eyes and dark hair.
His first name begins with an M and an I.

I sat eating dinner
When he spotted me
He came up and said,
'Will you go out with me?'
My face turned red and everyone stared.
I couldn't come out with the right word.

The answer was yes
Which he thought was a guess
On behalf of my lucky charms
With the wink of an eye
I went to fly into his loving arms.

Kayleigh Piper (11)
Frederick Gent School

The Night

A dark black night
whispering voices howling in the night wind.
A thin tall boy standing in the snow
up to his knees and covered in snow.
Standing near a gloomy house,
hearing voices in the night wind.
He was getting scared,
and shivering inside.
He was cold.

Rebecca Stacey Whitton (11)
Frederick Gent School

MY PHOTO

Sitting there,
Waiting, waiting.
The bell struck half past three,
I rushed off to the flowering tree.

Off we went,
To the video shop.
Was he ready
For us three?

We went up the stairs,
Slowly, cautiously.
Up we went,
Us three.

Yes, he was,
Wasn't he nice?
Who did he want?
Surely not me!

Sitting there,
Posing, posing.
How shall I pose?
What shall I wear?

I didn't know
Posing could be so much fun,
Especially when you're the one
Having the photograph done.

Amy Coleman (11)
Frederick Gent School

PROBLEM PARENTS

My parents are just, well crazy things,
In the middle of the street they start to sing,
It's embarrassing as they start to prance,
And do their loony, psycho dance.

They make my friends shake with laughter,
They go on about them for ages after,
I tell them they have a mental disorder,
And not to cross the bedroom border.

My mum says she used to be a star,
My dad says that he jumped so far,
That he was put in the Olympics,
Then crunches on several chocolate biscuits.

My dad plays Santa at Christmas time,
And makes up a crazy, whappy rhyme,
His dad did it to him as a boy,
He starts to play with my favourite toy.

My mum, she really is a prankster,
She says she used to be a gangster,
She worked in a club from dusk till dawn,
Until of course Lindsey was born.

They just can't help the way they are,
I'm glad really they're quite bizarre,
Because if they weren't that way you see,
Then maybe I wouldn't be me.

Katie Gaughan (11)
Frederick Gent School

SPACE

Stars shining bright,
They gleam like a light.
The sun as bright
As it will ever be,
Andromeda, who is she?
Orion, where's the car?
Pole, what is that?
Plough, where's the farmer?
The sun?
They must all be stars.
Stars shining bright,
They gleam like a light.
Stars, stars and more stars!
Stars shining bright,
They gleam like a light.

Ike Kirk (11)
Frederick Gent School

LONELY HEARTS

Sad and alone nobody to love and care for me.
Wandering the streets trying to answer the question
'Why me, why me?'
People used to love me and left me
to look after myself in every possible way.
There I lay, helpless in a sad way.
People pass, they know I feel hurt.
Why can't anyone help me?
Give me food and a nice hot bath.
My heart longs for love but in the end
all I am is alone, alone, alone.

Jade Rae (12)
Frederick Gent School

HALLOWE'EN

Witches, goblins lie in wait,
Watching close October's date.
Children clothed in fancy dress,
'Trick or treat' they shout in jest.

Pumpkins glowing in the dark,
Black capes flapping through the park.
Witching hour will soon be here,
Children's faces fill with fear.

The witch is followed by her cat,
As she makes a spell with a toad so fat.
The witches spell is strong, beware,
How easy do you scare?

Jemma Moss (11)
Frederick Gent School

MY FAMILY

My family is crazy
My family is mad
My stepdad is lazy
My little brother is bad

My mum cooks and cleans
My older sister is really mean
My puppy's dead sweet
And she likes a lot of wheat

My gran thinks I'm a brill child
But my mum thinks I'm wild
My grandad thinks I'm kind
But I know I've got a crazy mind.

Lucy Churm (12)
Frederick Gent School

EXPLORING THE STAFFROOM

We stand outside in snow and rain,
when the teachers are warm and cosy.
They sit with a nice cup of boiling hot coffee
and we got nothing!
50p for a can of coke that freezes your mouth when you sip it.
I've seen the cosy warm staffroom and
you wouldn't believe it unless you've seen it too.
There's toilets and sinks, tea machines, coffee machines,
everything, including a great cappuccino machine.
There's big comfy chairs that you sink into when you sit down.
There's big boxes of chocolates
and cooks being called for cakes,
but they're all very fattening.
Teachers tell us to be tidy,
but the staffroom is smelly and battered.
There's broken clocks and ripped letters
lying on floors and much, much more!

Amanda Ball (12)
Frederick Gent School

FAT MAT

My friend Mat is so, so fat
He eats all day and all night
He wakes to a very fat fright
Quick, put a lock on the fridge!
He is on a diet
He's keeping trim
He's keeping fit
But everyone knows it's not for long
Because it's teatime.

Wayne Mark Bearder (13)
Frederick Gent School

How Many Blades Of Grass?

The talented football player sprints down the pitch
He swerves past 20,000 blades of grass and then sees to an itch
The time runs closely to the end
The third official comes out and shows what he tends

The player strikes the opposition
As he plans to finish his mission
At the moment the score's a draw
But the crowd are wishing to end with more

What a through pass!
Just finish his task
The ball's in the back of the net!
The dumb goalkeeper has let

The ball went through his feet
The line to meet
Although it was a spectacular!
It just counts as a goal with no care

To celebrate his count
He counts all the mounts
Of blades of grass
And finishes his task
By kicking the ball into the crowd
When the ref blows his whistle proud.

Jonathan Sherwood (12)
Frederick Gent School

My Brother

My brother's football crazy.
My brother's football mad.
My brother hates daisies.
My brother is utterly lazy.

I know I drive him bonkers.
I know I drive him mad.
But he is the best brother
I could ever have.

Benn James (12)
Frederick Gent School

HATES AND LIKES

Clarkson speeds around in it
Rich people are found in it
TVRs (fast cars)
I like that stuff.

Old people slouch in it
Old spare wheels are found in it
Reliant Robins
I hate that stuff.

Sad people run in it
Smart people burn it
Aaagghh! shell suits
I absolutely *hate* that stuff.

People present on it
Sharp and Matsui make it
Television
I like that stuff.

Girls wear it - *yuk!*
It's gross, just the smell of it
Perfume
Yuk! Yuk! Yuk! I hate that stuff.

Joseph McEvoy (11)
Frederick Gent School

THE CAT

The cat's eyes seek revenge
on a helpless, cornered mouse.
The cat pounces with rage,
fur flying, mouse lays shattered.
No life, no hope . . . dead.
The cat comes in with so much glory,
lays down near the red sparks of the fire,
purring as I stroke his long
black, dusty, old fur coat.
The cat is now fast asleep
dreaming of his day.
He hears a noise,
jumps up, snarls.
Then upon all fours
as the other cat approaches,
seeking warmth and love.
He goes out later on,
he looks around his world
wondering what to do.
He sits upon the patio
staring up to the stars.
A moth circles up above
the cat dances round excitedly
and plays alongside the moth.
It falls dead.
He crosses the road.
Bang!
Remember curiosity killed
the cat.

Luke Townsend (12)
Frederick Gent School

NEVER UNDERSTOOD

You broke my heart when you said goodbye,
You didn't realise you made me cry.
You said you didn't love me any more,
From my eyes the tears did pour.
When I said 'I'll never forget the very
First day that we met.'
Then you turned round and hurt me most,
You leaned casually on the post.
About a new girl you did boast,
Her very own name you wouldn't say,
Then you were on your way,
Before I knew it,
By the window I did sit,
I watched you walk down the street.
I watched every movement of your feet.
I never understood your quick goodbye,
I'll never forget you till I die.

Hannah Parsons (12)
Frederick Gent School

THE SUN

The sun is round like a marble,
The colours in it look like flames.
The noise it makes is quite a barble,
The flames look like a horse's mane!

The sun is such a burning star,
It brightens up the world.
The way it moves is like a car,
The flicks of light are hurled.

Cheryl Payne (11)
Frederick Gent School

THEME PARK

Bang, whiz, the park has just opened.
People rush in like a herd of wild animals.
The children are screaming
while the grown-ups are eating.
The rides are all whizzing and
the stalls are all busy.
            Theme park.
The hot dogs are all steaming
and the ice-cream is gleaming.
As all the children are screaming
the ice-cream man is dealing,
while peeling his oranges ready
for his tea.

Louise Clamp (12)
Frederick Gent School

LOVE!

It was love at first sight
I didn't know then but I do now
He's got gorgeous brown hair
And dreamy green eyes
With his luscious pale pink lips
He's my kind of guy.

He's really quite funny when he wants to be
He's really kind and caring towards me
I smiled at him goofily the other day
I think he knows I like him
What will I do?

Jenny Spencer (12)
Frederick Gent School

A Close Friend

I have a friend called Emma
She lives so far away
I miss her all the time so much
She often comes to stay

We used to do so much together
Like dancing, singing and plays
We were together all the time
I loved our special days

She's funny, kind and pretty
She's got a heart of gold
I hope we're friends forever
Even when we're old

As time goes by I hope we'll be
As close as we can be
That distance doesn't spoil our friendship
We'll just have to wait and see.

Gemma Harshaw (12)
Frederick Gent School

War

Bombs, guns, people dying in my head.
Helpless children, no water, food or medicine.
Love can't be found in people's hearts.
Why can't I wake up one day
and find the war has gone away?

Jemma Luckett (12)
Frederick Gent School

BRAMBLE (1990-1996)

I feel alone now you've gone,
There will not be another one,
Who would listen to me like you used to,
Or cheer me up when I'm feeling blue.

I think of you in my mind,
A friend so tender, warm and kind,
But now you've gone,
I miss you so.

You'll never come back to visit me,
But just leave me here in misery,
I remember when we would walk together,
Through the trees, in and out of the heather.

A friend so dear and gentle to me,
A best friend you could ever be,
We buried you under the apple tree,
Flowers there for all to see.

A pretty face white, wiry hair,
You would run around, sit and stare,
Big brown eyes hard to handle,
My best friend, my dog Bramble.

Nicola Donson (12)
Frederick Gent School

BASKETBALL (IN THE GYM)

The ball is bouncing on the floor,
It is getting closer to the door,
Where the open hole awaits,
Just hoping the concentration will not break.

Yes and it is a goal,
I could do with a bowl (for my feet I mean)
Yes we won just by one,
But oh my God it was a close one.

Claire Ebbern (12)
Frederick Gent School

SHOOTING STARS

I don't know why I did it,
But I looked up in the sky,
And there up in the darkness,
A shooting star flew by.

It seemed to glide for miles,
With sparkles of white and blue,
I watched with great amazement,
And I knew just what to do.

My mamma always used to say,
'If you see a shooting star,
You close your eyes and make a wish,
And with luck you would go far!'

Depending what you wished for,
With luck it would come true,
Perhaps a house, a cat, or dog,
Or a jet ski painted blue.

I didn't wish for any of those!
You may just think I'm potty,
The only thing I really want,
Is for mum to win the lottery

Rebecca Jones (12)
Frederick Gent School

MY ATTIC

I'm walking up the creaky stairs,
I can hear the rats and mice,
I'm getting closer to the dark misty gloom,
I can feel the change in air,
What will it be like up there in the room?
I can smell all the dust waiting
To come at me in a gust,
It's large and creepy,
I can see all the dead spiders and young rats,
I've only been up here twice,
Once with my grandma and
Now on my own.

Lyndsey Cleaver (12)
Frederick Gent School

THE BOY

I see him across the street
With the Kappa trainers on his feet
He's cute, he's cool
He's making me feel a fool
I see him walking head held high
I can't help but stare when he goes by

I just think he's really fit
I wish I could see him in his football kit
But life's not fair, so I've been told
So I'll have to watch him from across the road.

Lisa Parsley (12)
Frederick Gent School

SPACEMAN ALEC

Exploring is fun most of the time
Let's explore the third kind:
Racing through space at terrific pace
Spaceman Alec is on the case.

Aliens! Where? Over there,
Eating his lunch on the revolving chair
What's in his lunch box or on his bread?
If you don't be careful it could be your head!'

Quick don't run, get out your gun
Blast this thing towards the sun
Let's carry on, space is exciting
But moments like that make it
A wee bit frightening.

James Turner (12)
Frederick Gent School

MY ENGLISH TEACHER MR CLAMP

My English teacher
Mr Clamp
Went bonkers every time
I pulled a prank
It's Lee stand up
And put your hands on your head.
Lee, stand in the corner.
Lee, do you want a break time?
Lee, do you want a dinner time?
Lee, do you want to come back at 3.25?

Lee Berry (12)
Frederick Gent School

DESPAIR

Why have the right to discriminate and shame people,
Of which you don't even know a name,
Single parent families of which there is a lot,
Fight to keep their children, some win and some do not.

Poor and homeless people who really need our help,
No one seems to care or will tighten up their belt,
Starving Biafran children who haven't ate in days,
Water is their lifeline please give what you can save.

Rainforests dying at an increasing speed,
We don't have the sense to look after what we need,
The millennium approaches faster every day,
Will the earth live to see it?
Well only God can say.

Lauren May Hawkins (13)
Frederick Gent School

BULLY BY NAME, BULLY BY NATURE

Bully by name, bully by nature,
There's no excuse.

Bully by name, bully by nature,
Why do you hurt me, with abuse?

Bully by name, bully by nature,
Why do you get me, without dismay?

Bully by name, bully by nature,
Find a heart, and go away!

Ian Graney (13)
Frederick Gent School

MA, CAN I GO OUT?

Ma, can I go out?
No shouts me dad
Ye shouts me ma
It's all the same
Every time I wanna go out

Ma, can I go out?
No!
I don't know why
She won't let me out

Maybe she's scared
Maybe she's heard
I don't know why
Every time I wanna go out
She always says
       No!

Sarah Hallam (11)
Frederick Gent School

PARENTS

'What shall I do with this?'
'What shall I do with that?'
'What is this and what is that?'
'Shut up sit down
Or go to bed before I hit you round the head'
'Do your homework, help your father'
'Cook us dinner'
'Make it a winner.'

Matthew Vitel (11)
Frederick Gent School

A War Game Gone Wrong

'It's a war game gone wrong,' said the commander,
As he lined up his troops on the front line
Preparing to engage the enemy with one
Last attempt at victory.
But to his dismay the enemy they all so much
Feared attacked from behind.
'Arthur's hit' yelled a voice form the back,
'He's been shot in the back by a shell' said another.

He passed away later that day no matter
How much they all prayed.

A special burial was performed later that
Day to mark the life and death of a special
Victim of war.

Paul Marriott (15)
Frederick Gent School

My Worm Wayne!

My worm Wayne was a terrible pain,
he wiggled and slithered all over the place.

I could never find him because I couldn't see his face,
that worm called Wayne of mine.

You could guarantee always and every time
he would find his way round to my bed and
pretend to be dead,
that worm called Wayne of mine!

Joe Gillam (12)
Frederick Gent School

HILL HAUNTING

I stood at the top of the hill,
With all the sheep looking on,
And I slipped and I fell and I fell until
I dropped on the ground and was gone.

So now I haunt that terrible hill,
With contempt for any who can,
Climb up and down it with the skill,
Of any hill walking fan.

I try to push people off the end,
In my hope to find,
A wonderful, caring assistant and friend,
Who'll share haunting shifts and won't mind.

But I'm not getting very far,
'Cos no one comes near here.
'Though my story's made me a superstar,
It fills everybody with fear.

Because they don't want to be killed,
Which they know they will be,
If they come near my hill,
'Cos they'll be pushed off the end . . .
By me!

Eloise Hopkinson (12)
Frederick Gent School

TANGO

Tango is my new mare
Playing in the field so bare
She's lively when she wants to be
She moves so fast she's hard to see.

Tango is my new mare
Trotting proudly hoping you'll stare
Our biggest aim is to be the best
And win all the rosettes, we'll beat the rest.

Tango is my new mare
So clean and bright, she is
And when she jumps
She has to whiz.

Tango is my new mare
With a black mane and tail
I definitely wouldn't put her up for sale
She eats one bale of hay a day
That's a lot some people say.

Tango is my new mare
She loves to play which gives her a flare
But there's one thing I have to say
. . . I love her.

Joanne Coope (12)
Frederick Gent School

MAX!

Max is my dog
And he's really, really sweet
He does all kinds of tricks
Which are really, really neat.

He sits, stays, lies down and barks
When someone walks up the path
And when he chases after his tail
He really makes us laugh!

When you're eating breakfast
And eating tea at night
Max comes to sit beside you
And eats everything in sight

He can sometimes be friendly
He can sometimes be a pain
And when he starts to bite you
He thinks it's just a game.

My dog Max is really cute
We're happy as can be
Especially when he's fast asleep
But I know he'll always love me.

Laura Mills (12)
Frederick Gent School

FOOTBALL

Football, football, what a name
Football, football, what a game
Fans form a queue outside the ground
Then watch the seconds tick around
It's nearly time, the gates unlock
The kick off's here, it's 3 o'clock

The whistle blows, the ball is kicked
from one player to another
They try and try to score a goal
I wonder why they bother

90 minutes running around getting hot and sweaty
And all the referee can do is be rather petty

The game is nice fun for all
But I can't say because I'm the ball.

Peter Fritchley (12)
Frederick Gent School

SNAKES

Snakes are multicoloured,
They slither and they slide.
Some like to attack you,
And some they just hide.

Snakes eat their food alive,
They like birds, rats and mice.
Their jaw drops down and gulps whole,
And crushes its prey in a trice.

There are many different snakes,
Some are poisonous, some are not.
Some will just strangle you,
Some will blind you with venom which is hot.

There are big ones, fat ones, thin ones and there are long ones,
Some even live in the sea.
I don't care where they live really,
So long as they don't live near me.

Jade Brown (12)
Frederick Gent School

I CAN'T STOP WRITING POEMS!

I can't stop writing poems,
        I don't know when to stop,
I can't stop writing poems,
        My pen's about to pop!

        I write them in the morning,
                I write them last thing at night,
        My teacher's very pleased with me,
                But sadly, I'm not that bright!

        I write them when I'm reading,
I write them when I'm dreaming,
        I write them when I'm eating,
I write them everywhere.

        I'm going to talk to Mr Clamp,
                See if I can talk to his wife,
        But one thing I've got to ask you is this,
                Mr Clamp, what have you done to my brain?

Emily Michelle Martin (11)
Frederick Gent School

THEN I AWOKE

I'm sailing on a boat
A million miles from home
Just like the Titanic, I saw an iceberg
I couldn't miss it, crash!
The boat went down
I chucked off my gown
And started to swim
The outlook was dim
After hours I found land
In the sand I found a silver coin
Then I saw a man shouting
'Give me the coin boy!'
He caught me
He put his hands around my neck
I couldn't breath
I began to choke
Then I awoke.

Ben Eveson (12)
Frederick Gent School

THE WAY I LIKE TO THINK

I like to think of Saturday
When I go away from school
I'll catch the train
And fly to Spain
I'll never go to school again
I'll sail the sea
I'll fly in the sky
I'll even win the lottery
I'll . . . 'Adam, get on with your work!'
But that's the way I like to think.

Adam Whatton (12)
Frederick Gent School

WHEN I WENT TO THE ZOO
AND EXPLORED

When I went to the zoo
I saw and was amazed,
By a large giraffe,
With a long neck,
A panda,
With black and white patches,
I was amazed by how they behave.

Then I saw the monkeys
Swinging from tree to tree,
I explored their fine brown coat,
And their long tail.

The hippos were having a bath,
The tigers were cleaning their teeth,
Licking their chops for some British meat.

The pigs were grunting,
And rolling in mud,
The goats were eating my hair,
Getting ready for some lunch.

Then I saw some ducks,
They were quacking,
The hens were clucking,
The snakes were hissing
So I started to sing
And it rained.

My mum got wet
She didn't have a hood,
So she told me to go,
To the car,
Then we went home.

Nicola Jane Wyldbore (12)
Frederick Gent School

THE TEACHERS' STAFFROOM

One night last week I took a sneaky peep in the teachers' staffroom,
It's like where a bear lives, it's like a tomb!
There's coffee stains on the table, there's mess on the floor,
I looked and saw a piece of paper of how the school was a bore!
I saw a mattress, it was as comfy as a bed,
Squashed down the side was Miss' cigarette!
I found a vodka bottle and upon it said a name,
'Miss Flame!'
On the wall a photograph of Mr Lesley,
He was dressed up as Elvis Presley!
Again I looked around and saw a wig on a stand,
It belonged to none other than Mr Strand!
I know this may seem crazy,
But then I saw a crying baby!
Up pulled a Rover,
And out climbed Mrs Esenover!
It's a shame to go but someday I'll be back,
To where the teachers just lie and *slack!*

Emma Stones (11)
Frederick Gent School

GRANDMAS

Grandmas are very annoying,
They think that we just play the fool.
They sit there moaning and groaning,
They never just sit and act cool.

I ran to the kitchen to get away from her
And then I heard the old bat shout,
'Bring my false teeth, they're in a small jug
And hurry you small little trout.'

Her false teeth sat bobbing in a rotted old jug,
All the back teeth were filled up with mud.
She couldn't even keep her false teeth clean,
She had never wanted teeth that would gleam.

I picked out the teeth with a finger and thumb
And longed for the moment when I would be done.
I threw them at Grandma then ran out the door,
I was never going there anymore.

Vicki Gibson (11)
Frederick Gent School

DAYDREAMIN' (A SONG)

In my head there is a picture,
Of what it used to be,
I'll never forget the way it was,
Or how we used to be.
I remember thinking will this ever end,
Or when's it gonna stop?
'Cause in my heart it will never end,
And in my head it will go on and on,
Forever.

Oh in my head I'm on a rocket to the moon,
Stranded on an island and I'm on a shooting star.
I'm under the sea with all the fishes
Collecting seashells big and small.

In my head I hear a buzzing bee,
Going on and on, I'm in a field so far away
And I'm not coming back for the rest of today
'Cause I'm daydreamin'

Katie Rogers (11)
Frederick Gent School

FROST PICTURES

In winter jumping from my bed,
To part my curtains blue and red,
To see upon the windowpane
A frosty fairyland again.

As though a secret magic hand,
Had painted there a wonderland,
Of frozen ferns and castles tall,
And sparkling flowers, large and small.

But when the sun begins to rise,
With beams so dazzling to my eyes,
The magic pictures quickly pass,
And just leave water on the grass.

Stacey Smalley (12)
Frederick Gent School

IN MY HEAD

I think of loads of things,
I dream to be a king,
Ruling England
Fighting in battles,
Riding a horse with a big flag in my hand
Riding it on bright yellow sand,
With a great big band behind me,
I wear a big red cloak,
A great big yellow circle in the middle,
Which is like a great big egg yolk.

Nicholas Walters (11)
Frederick Gent School

LIVERPOOL

Look at Owen go,
Past one defender,
Past another,
Isn't he brilliant
Oh no!
He's lost the ball
He's got it back again
In it goes
Goal!

Robbie Fowler is the best
He's the one with all the zest
There it goes again
In the top left corner
Goal!

Lauren England (12)
Frederick Gent School

THE FOOL SCHOOL

I'm exploring this great new school,
I walk into the wrong class, I'm called a fool.
I say, 'It takes one to know one.'
They say, 'We know, as it's the fool school.'
'Fool school,' I say in my head.
'Hey you want a tenner?' says Fred.
'A tenner,' I said in my head.
'Sure giz it,' I said.
'No way,' said Fred
And punched me in the nose
This school is a fool don't come here to
Doom! Doom! Doom!

Adam Reville (12)
Frederick Gent School

TEAR OF TRUE LOVE!

Tears of true love,
Fell from my cheeks,
As the years hopes and dreams
Relieved from midsummer weeks.
My love for you,
Poured out from my eyes
And all of the clichés,
And all of the lies
And all of the space,
I needed from you
Closer, then further,
Then closer drew!

The river we loved,
And the one for which we once cared
Held secrets, but telling them,
No longer dared.
Your heart it held,
And captured mine
But blind was I,
I didn't see the sign.
I should have seen,
You were dying inside,
When all the while,
I was trying to hide
From love . . .

Megan L Walters (12)
Frederick Gent School

Us In 8N!

Us in 8N
Are really quite noisy,
Us in 8N,
Are really quite nice,
Us in 8N,
Are really quite funky,
Us in 8N,
Really like to rap.

Some of us in 8N,
Are really quite naughty,
Some of us in 8N,
Are quite the average person,
And the others,
Well are really just plain mad.

Laura Bednarz (12)
Frederick Gent School

Witches

This is the night when witches fly.
On their broomsticks
whizzing through the sky.
Up and up they fly so high.
Why oh why do witches fly.

Bats and rats and lizards too.
All go in to make a witches' brew
They stir and stir to mix it up
Then serve it out and eat it up.

Rachel Rawson (12)
Frederick Gent School

MY FAMILY AND FRIENDS

My family are very kind and helpful.
My dad says kind things about me.
My mum says kind and happy things about me.

My pets are three cats, one dog, thirteen fish,
One hamster, one rabbit.
They are fluffy and sweet loving and friendly.

My friends are caring, loving and kind.
I have lots of new friends from Pixiton.
I am still friends with the ones from the Glebe.
But there are two people now I am not friends with.
I like being at Frederick Gent School.
They have everything.

Melissa Shields (11)
Frederick Gent School

CLAMPY

Our English teacher is Mr Clamp.
Did you know it rhymes with lamp
And also amp.
Spellings once a week.
And maybe a dictionary race.
How can we keep up this pace.
All this once a week.
The ending is so bleak.
How will we survive?
Will we get out alive?

Jamie Bunting (12)
Frederick Gent School

EXPLORING THE WORLD

The frogs are jumping,
The grass is green,
The sun is shining on the trees that gleam.

The sea is running,
The seagulls are alive,
The dolphins are jumping in and out of a bowl of wine.

The elephants are charging,
The giraffes are alive,
The lions and tigers are having a meeting.

The cows are mooing
The horses are neighing,
The sheep are bleating and the chicks are tweeting.

The llamas are spitting,
The hyenas are laughing,
The bars are rattling as the chimps are chattering.

Carla Ryntowt (12)
Frederick Gent School

GRAVEYARD

G raves wearing with the wind.
R aving trees swaying side to side.
A pples falling on the cracked path
V ery young and old people live there
E verybody goes there in the end.
Y elling people, yelling, 'Why?'
A little boy not understanding why.
R ose petals on the floor as a red carpet
D eath is dark and gloomy but we all have to go.

Kayleigh Blythe (13)
Frederick Gent School

FROM A FAMILY PHOTO

On the beach in the sun
My sister and brother were having fun
Collecting shells
Paddling in the sea
They really liked it. Yippee!

Building sandcastles, loads of laughs
Making footprints like little paths.
They didn't want to come home,
They would rather stay alone -
And that was their day at the beach.

Tara Graney (11)
Frederick Gent School

MICHAEL OWEN

There he was in his flashing suit,
Oh, in that suit he looked so cute.
Down the pitch like the wind he ran,
As only Michael Owen can.
His hair gleaming brown,
He never had a frown.
Oh what a goal,
He then made a roll.
With his sweaty shirt over his head,
He ran around and bumped his head,
'Oh Michael,' the girls said.

Nicole Atkinson (11)
Frederick Gent School

THOUGHTS?

Round the last defender
With thoughts running through
My head.
Where shall I put the ball
Apart from the net?
What if I miss?
The pressure is really on.
For me to score
Or my heart will not go on.

Robert Cairns (12)
Frederick Gent School

THE MAGIC BOX

The magic box, what could it be?
A secret thing lying within me,
All my love, hope and cares.

The big gold box is really my life
From the first day at school to when I shall marry.
Heartache and death from tears then to laughter.
With all my life hope and cares and everything else
I know I am safe inside.

Kirsty Atherton (11)
Frederick Gent School

WHY?

What is life?
Where does it come from?
Where does it go?
What's the point?
Is there one?
Do I have a point in life?
Does anyone?

What is everything made of?
Where does everything come from?
Where does everything go?
Can something come from nothing?
Something must have done mustn't it?
What are things?
Do dead things die?

What is time?
Where does it come from?
Where does it go?
Can time stop?
Will it stop?
Does anyone know?
I don't know why?

Liz Smith (12)
Frederick Gent School

A SINGLE FROZEN NIGHT

The snow shone like it was a carpet of fire,
Looking up into the sky of nothingness,
The moon stood out like a single white tooth,
But it was cold, cold as fear.

Then the snowflakes fell,
Shaped as delicately as the icing on a wedding cake,
As they landed on the ground they fuelled the brightness,
The scene was like it had been put under the same spell as Narnia.

It was silent, like the world had been frozen,
And then, the moon began to fade,
In its place the sun appeared,
More powerful and radiant,
As its beams lit the sky.

Alice Jane Milner (12)
Highfields School

THE CHANGING SEASONS

Today the sun is shining,
All around the leaves are turning,
Lovely shades of green to gold,
Soon the frost will come,
All the leaves will come falling down,
Drifting to the ground
And coat the floor in a beautiful carpet,
The most colourful to be found,
The leaves have gone, the trees are bare,
Soon to be coated in frost's icy glare.

Charlotte Fletcher (13)
Highfields School

A FLEETING MOMENT

The world lies white and still,
Its outlines blurred and smoothed
Beneath the shrouds of winter.
No wind stirs the falling flakes
Which softly descend
In dizzying, endless multitudes.
The silence overwhelms,
Its presence enormous, tangible,
White and devoid as the vacuous landscape.
No movement breaks the spell
Of silence and of stillness,
Deafening in their intensity.
The world lies submerged beneath
A deep, unfathomable ocean,
Not even the slightest sound
Sends ripples across its glassy surface.
Only the endless spiralling flakes
Give a sense of passing time.
The endless, repeated monotony
Entrances, almost hypnotic
In its empty, ageless power.
This fleeting moment,
A time of utter calm and silence
Lies, forever present,
Imprinted on the mind.

Edmund Hunt (15)
Highfields School

THE GHOST

Did anyone see that ghost over there?
The man asked with fear in his heart
So everyone turned
Just to find that there was no one there.

The ghost, the ghost his footsteps are nearing you
Turn and you see that no one is there.

Did anyone hear those footsteps creaking?
She cried in fright to them all
So everyone screamed
They did not know he was watching them all.

The ghost, the ghost his footsteps are nearing you
Turn and you see that no one is there.

Does anyone smell that strange musty smell?
They asked as they crept up the stairs
They all stepped back
As they came face to face with their ghost.

The ghost, the ghost his footsteps are nearing you
Turn and you see that no one is there.

The ghost.
The ghost.
The ghost.
The ghost.

Danielle Crawford (12)
Highfields School

SIX SPOTTED EGGS

Out of the blue the island fell,
darkened by an evil spell.
The blink of an eye is all it took
and the island became a story book.
The super-happy tree went too,
at once the yoshis began to stew.
Only baby Bouser could be so mean
to spoil the happy yoshis' dreams.
But far away upon the isle
some yoshi eggs survived the trial.
The spotted eggs began to hatch,
six little yoshis - a perfect batch.
They scratched their heads and looked around,
some even tried to pound the ground.
Sadness darkened every yoshi's face
It should have been a super-happy place.
The yoshis knew what was a hand,
And began to plot a cunning plan.
Their mission then was crystal clear
They had to go and spread the cheer.
They set out to follow the fruit
To find where the tree had taken root.

Grant Baynes (11)
Highfields School

FRIENDS

Friends are there for you no matter what,
Even though we argue, and that we do a lot,
People say we're mad arguing over nothing,
But in the bright lights
We party all night
And fall out about absolutely nothing.

You can talk to them about anything,
Anything at all.
You can tell them your secrets
And you don't have to worry at all.
You can have friends as boys
But sometimes it depends
On whether they are gonna grow up
And mature and be your boyfriends.

Amy Oldershaw (13)
Highfields School

MONDAY

7 am the alarm clock sounds,
Monday morning starts.
Dog's first up, roaming free,
No one else around.

Next on the scene is Mum,
Proud, prim and proper.
Rounding up the kids one by one,
Not always with success.

Breakfast time, disaster zone.
Sulky, sullen family.
Cereal on homework, tea on shirt,
What will happen next?

Ten to nine, is that the time!
Shoes, coat and hat.
'I've missed my bus!' 'My car won't start!'
Monday morning news.

Naomi Smallman (13)
Highfields School

SUMMER HAS ENDED

The nights are drawing in heralding autumn's beginning.
No more long summer days,
Laughing and joking with my friends till late.
No more of the sun's powerful rays
No more sweltering days
Summer has ended.
The flowers that once held their heads up high
Are bowed and dying.
The birds congregate in readiness for their long journey.
The days are growing colder
Summer has ended.
Misty morning and watery sunlight
Changing colours from green to golds, to reds to browns.
Autumn has its own special beauty
But summer has ended.

Rupert Hoskin (13)
Highfields School

ONE COLOURFUL DAY

Listen to the sound of the rustling leaves
Watch a bee fly past a buzzing hive
Water running down the river in all shapes and colours
Nice big fish swimming around in shoals.

A rainbow shining over the hills
The smoke being puffed out by the mills
Then the rain comes out and waters the plants
A dead rat is found by the searching ants.

Chris Roberts (13)
Highfields School

WHEN THE SPRING COMES

I adore it when the spring starts to come
The warm days bring out children and the sun.
Whilst the nights show stars sparkling in the sky,
I lie there staring as life passes me by.

Little newborn lambs jump around the fields
As their mums and dads scavenge for their meals
Little chicks hatch out of stuffy eggs.
They are small, pink and bare with little legs.

Springtime means Easter is drawing near
Families buy lots of chocolate which is dear.
But another message has to be told
And it's about Jesus when he arose.

When I think what I did this time last year
I remember how we had to clear
All those brown leaves which fall at wintertime
And now that's the end of our little rhyme.

Sarah Whittington (13)
Highfields School

THE SOUNDS OF NIGHT

Lying snug in my sleeping bag,
Safe inside my tent,
My torch glimmers with a yellow glow as the batteries fade,
I am alone in the night,
But the night is full of sound.
The wind rustles the leaves on the trees,
An owl shrieks from its perch,
Bats twitter as they swoop between their beams,
Slowly I drift away until the morning chorus awakens me.

Adam Varkalis (12)
Highfields School

MY DOG JACK

He is black, white and furry,
He wakes up very early.

He'll go outside for a quick walk,
Then comes inside to wake me up.

He'll wait for the postman for the mail,
When he comes he'll wag his tail.

While I'm at school he'll rest all day,
Just waiting for me to come home and play.

His favourite game is tug of war,
He wants to play it more and more.

He'll lie down not to make a peep,
Before you know it he's fast asleep.

Sam Blood (13)
Highfields School

SPRING MORNING

I wake up in the morning
To the sound of birds singing
On the telephone line outside my window.

I get up to look out of the window
And I can see the rabbits playing.
The squirrels are inquisitively looking round for nuts,
They are fresh out of hibernation.

The birds are gathering sticks and fluff
To build their nests
Ready for their young that are on the way.

James White (13)
Highfields School

CLOUDS

They come from nowhere
Drifting in the sky
Peering down on the world
From up on high.

They carry the rain
To water the ground
They move on slowly
Without a sound.

White and fluffy
Or black and grey
They can spoil a picnic
Or make your day.

They're in the sky
From dawn till dusk
A sunset can turn them
The colour of rust.

Steve Hicklin (13)
Highfields School

FROM MY WINDOW

As I sit by my window looking up the valley,
I can see the black clouds coming close.
The wind starts to blow the trees.
I look again, now the raindrops come.
The cattle come down from grazing to shelter.
Now the rain comes to a stop.
Up the valley I see a rainbow
Coming from the clouds the sun peeps out
All looking clean fresh and still up the valley.

James Wardman (12)
Highfields School

ME!

I like me
I like my age
I'm not too old
I'm not too young
To
Stand on my head
Swing on the railings
Yell all day and get my own way
Or I can
Spend hours in the shopping centre,
getting rid of hundreds of pounds
Or years in the bathroom putting the
finishing touches to my face.
Spend all day, dreaming about *him!*
And nobody is at all surprised!

Claire Drinkall (11)
Highfields School

THE BEAST

Its pointy
eyes searching
for its feast.
Slinky movements calm and
lazy, it pauses.
Watching and searching.
Searching for its feast.
Carefully moving, slouching side to side
Waiting sneakily for its feast.

Becki Burrell (12)
Highfields School

CROMFORD - THEN AND NOW

I sit here looking through the window
A view from past to present
Ahead old houses built by Arkwright
Built for the first of the world's workers
Below a pond to power his mill
A waterwheel turns gently
Two swans glide gently upon the shiny water
Three chapels I see
How peaceful it must of been
All this set upon a sea of green
But wait, I now see the modern village
Motorbikes, lorries and cars killing the silence
The stone is carried from the local quarry.
Gaping holes cut into the countryside
I see little brick boxes - the modern houses
Traffic lights flashing, crossings bleeping.
I hear sirens sounding, people rushing cars parking everywhere
If this is how it's meant to be
What can we expect from the next century?

Adam Ward (13)
Highfields School

MEGAN

My dog Megan, has big brown eyes
Turning happy and mournful
We don't know why.

She squeaks with joy, when we enter the door,
Busying round, she always wants more
She plays like a puppy, eats like a horse
But we all love her, of course.

Bryony Stevens (13)
Highfields School

GRAND PRIX

He's in the car for the big race,
On the warm up lap just to get in place.
Once again he's in pole position,
To win this race is his mission.
Anxiously waiting for the green lights to come
He sits there listening to his engine hum.
The red lights go out and turn into green,
He shoots off the line almost unable to be seen.
The crowd all cheering,
At all the braking and steering.
Accelerating on every straight,
At the corners he's braking late.
Now he's just gone into the lead,
In front of the grandstand at full speed.
The crew are signalling for a pit stop,
A quick tyre change and out, still on top.
Split seconds only separate them
The crowd cheering for both men.
In and out fast and slow,
No way past, nowhere to go.
Into the 'SS', hard on the brakes.
Exits the corner and accelerates.
In his mirror the sky is black
A cloud of smoke as his rival drops back.
Once again he's out on his own
The track is clear he's all alone.
On the last lap racing clear,
No one to touch him, no one to fear.
He races past the chequered flag,
First position in the bag.
Spraying champagne on the crowd
National anthems play out loud.

Daniel Johnson (12)
Highfields School

GOING CAMPING

We pack our car
Getting ready for afar
The tent, four sleeping bags
Making sure nothing lags.

Along the motorway we drive
Its lanes vast and wide
We drive through the port
Seeing boats of every sort
We come to ours at last
Enormous, it's a ferry without a mast.

Eventually we arrive at France
In a good and very relaxed stance
On we go to our campsite
Get there before tea? We might
We take all the fast French main roads
But we didn't see any French toads.

At the campsite we get shown our places
Enthusiasm on our faces
We set up tent for the night
Into big France we journey at
First light.

David Hayward (13)
Highfields School

SNOW

Slowly drifting to the floor,
Carpeting the streets as it falls.
Each flake glistening like a diamond in the moon,
Slowly drifting to the floor.

Christy Britland (13)
Highfields School

THE CAT

The cat was feeling very bored,
He'd played with all of his toys,
The ball of string, the rubber mouse,
And the ball that makes a noise.

He thought he'd go outside,
To see what he could see,
Then he saw a little bird,
And chased it up a tree.

The bird went out of sight,
He started to go back down,
But it gave him a fright,
He daren't go up or down.

He started to miaow,
But then along came Tim,
Tim climbed up the tree,
And gently rescued him.

Lucy Brameld (13)
Highfields School

THE BARN OWL

The barn owl flies at night,
Its eyes gleam so bright.
Frosted rings around the moon,
The owl hoots its special tune.
Its darkening shadow in the moonlight's ray,
It's a nocturnal animal, sleeps all day.
Special feathers make it silently fly,
To help it swoop gracefully across the sky.

Lyndsay Broome (13)
Highfields School

THE GARDEN AT NIGHT

The garden at night
Gives me a fright
The noise of the fox
Makes me shiver in my socks
The screech of the owl
Whilst the wild dogs growl
The yell of a small bee wanting a slug
Or even a little juicy bug
The noise of cats and rats
Looking for some juicy snacks
The noise of TV coming from next door
Flying around is a little Jackdaw
When the sun finally comes up
All the animals go back to their huts.

James McElvaney (13)
Highfields School

THE FAIR

Noises fill the town and the lights shine in the dark,
People's screaming voices of laughter fill the night air.

Pink fluffy candyfloss and toffee apples too,
Sticky fingers everywhere,
The smell of hot dogs fill the air.

Everybody slowly starts to leave,
With empty pockets and spinning heads,
Everything has calmed down,
The fair is finally dead.

Holly Kirkland (13)
Highfields School

FRANCE

France is really very hot,
When I was there I swam a lot.
I swam in the pool, I swam in the sea,
But always made sure I was back for tea.

In the pool there was a slide,
And a safe place for me to dive.
But when I was in the sea,
Little fish kept chasing me!

We wandered around the pretty towns,
And heard lots of foreign sounds.
'Bonjour. Merci,' was all I could say,
But I'd soon learnt more by the end of the day.

In our tent we had a mouse,
It must have thought it was its house.
It woke up eating our food,
My sister thought it was very rude.

So to an end our holiday came,
Back to England and its rain!

Charlotte Liddicot (12)
Highfields School

NIGHTLIFE

Time is getting on
Darkness is falling
Energy's lost
New reality's found

The nightlife is starting
As tiredness looms
A bark of a dog
The hum of a car
The fairground rides from afar

Everything's still
Dreamland's in wait
Still I sit watching
Drunken people, passers by
From downstairs a cry

It's not so dark now
I'm used to the gloom
I draw in the blanket
Morning is coming
Too soon.

Jennifer Arran (13)
Highfields School

SOUNDS OF THE CITY

The sounds of the city are constant and droning,
They never stop day and night.
The thud of people's feet pulsating like a heartbeat,
The hum in cheap cafes of bright neon lights.

The clicking of cash tills,
The screeching of brakes,
An ambulance racing
And the sound that it makes.

The atmosphere is humid,
Bodies packed together, sardines in a tin,
A never ending stream of people,
Life, in many forms trapped within.

Jessica Inglis (13)
Highfields School

COME ON LEEDS

'Come on Leeds, here we go',
The fans sway their arms to and fro.
Their shirts different colours - yellow, white and blue,
They are the Leeds fans through and through.
The opposing fans in their shores of red,
Scarves on their necks, hats on their heads.
The atmosphere's great, I'm overawed,
It can be better than this I have been told.

Suddenly a great move, that started from far,
A thirty yard shot that just hit the bar.
He hits in the rebound, a player stops it by hand,
The ref looks hard then with firmness points to the ground.
Up steps a player with a smug looming grin,
He can see the keeper looking fiercely at him.
Cool as a crystal, he gives the ball an almighty whack,
It hits the top corner with a thudding smack.
Off runs the goal scorer with a triumphant roar,
What a great time, great moment to score.

Michael Williamson (13)
Highfields School

ABANDONED

Abandoned, left alone
Cold and shivering
Lonely and sad
Woof! His cry weakens
Woof!
All he needs is someone to
Find and give him a warm
Loving and caring home.

Melanie Keep (11)
Highfields School

TIGERS IN DANGER

Its glossy coat so soft and smooth,
Its striped body motionless,
            camouflaged.
It watched in the gentle, waving grass
As time ticks away.
Then *zoom!*
The tiger dashes towards its prey.
The horrified victim looks up,
Turns on its tail and flees.
But the tiger is too fast for it,
And catches its food as it darts
            towards the trees.
So why do we have to hunt it
            to extinction?
Not for food, just greed.

Kate Smith (12)
Highfields School

DICK THE DOLPHIN

Dick the dolphin loved to be
following the ships at sea.
People standing at the rail
saw his head and then his tail.
As Dick jumped up with grace
a fishy smile upon his face.
Then with a final jump he
left them all with one final
            flip.

Adrienne Wood (12)
Highfields School

FLOWERS

Flowers, flowers all around
Not a noise, not a sound
Reds, blues, yellows, greens
Oranges, pinks, blacks and
Creams
All the colours you would have seen
On the flowers they would have been
1 pound, 2 pound they are a bunch
Animals, insects will have a munch
Gardens, parks, fields they be
In Garden Weekly on TV
In pots, beds, toilets too
All on show for me and you
Autumn and winter they hibernate
Spring and summer they all look great.

Aaron Brough (12)
Highfields School

CONFUSED

Aunties, uncles,
Sisters, brothers,
Where do they all come from?

Birds and the bees my mother says,
My friends say it's not done!

How could birds and bees do that?
I do not understand,
I'll just have to wait, till I do this at school,
And that's what I demand!

Layla Fern (14)
Highfields School

THE TRICK

I felt crooked afterwards, and thought I would evermore.
It was cruel, malicious, but if I wanted to join I had to.
The guys dared me, they provoked me, so I did it.

I began to dig the trench, deeper, darker and meaner.
I then half filled it with my dad's fishing maggots.
The guilt sweating out of my forehead, I poured in the last box.

The others crawling about with laughter,
Watching me lay on all of the sticks,
Strong ones, weak ones, a smile was forming on my face.

I laid on the last stick and put on some grotty old turf.
The pit was now most camouflaged, and the leaves finished it off.
My feeble smile was now a full strength grin.

The others hid behind the bush, I checked and it was half four,
Just in time for Dwayne to walk past.
'Look here!' I shouted. 'Look here! I want to show you something.'

He came, a guilty frown entered my face.
It worried me, but it drew him closer and then it happened,
I fell down screaming with laughter.

Behind the bush they must have had stitches with laughing so much.
The expression on his face was telling you the maggots
Were in his clothes, squashed in his trainers.

Splattered maggots was a revolting sight, but unfortunately
Dwayne was boiling with anger, hatred and climbed out.
Chasing me through the woods, the others ran in different directions
Shouting out 'Well done, welcome to the group!'

Matthew Statham (13)
Highfields School

THE WHITE BEAR

Your captivating look is so fiercely enchanting,
But behind your soft complexion you are a vicious beast.
Powerful and strong with your huge soft paws,
Like a well worn leather rag.
Claws as sharp as pincers.
The legs that support your towering body,
So huge they remind me of velvet girders.
Way above the imagination of people,
You are the monster of snow.

You have a monochrome existence.
White on black,
Black on white.
Your life far beyond mankind.
Your ancestors the grizzly black and brown.
You are the monster of snow.
The polar bear.

Laura Sandner (14)
Highfields School

ALONE

I sit, I stare, I wonder
in the crowded deafening rabble,
I sit there, alone.
In 1510, at the clattering merry banquet,
I sit there, alone.
In the burning building, the difference
between life and death,
I sit there, alone.
Are there 1,000,000 people in this
world or am I . . . alone?

Gemma Fozzard (12)
Highfields School

TRILLION

Trillion is our little cat,
A long haired, fluffy thing,
And when she's sleeping on my bed,
I use her soft body as a pillow for my head!

Trillion gives us presents of dead mice and shrews,
We are so happy together.

One day Trillion appeared to have changed,
Hiding, frightened, in dark, dark places,
Trying to get away from the light,
Which seemed to torture her.

We took Trillion to the vet,
We knew she would have an evil time.
My family and I never adored Trillion,
As much as we did then.

She's better now.
You never realise how much you love someone
Until you think you might lose them.

Elizabeth Tunna (12)
Highfields School

THE MYSTERY HORSE

Galloping across the sands
Dashing over the lands
No cares in the world has my four legged-friend
No message did he send
He's a very beautiful creature
But he's got one very special feature
That being, he does not answer back.

Nicola Robinson (11)
Highfields School

RUGBY

Rugby is my favourite sport
I think it's really good
My favourite thing is scoring tries
And falling in the mud

My best position is scrum half
It really is quite great
I like to tackle people
And pass to all my mates

Racing down the centre
Pass out to the wing
Dive over the try line
Scoring is the thing

Make a tunnel clap your hands
Cheer the others through
Dive into the showers
We've won by 32.

James Pearson (12)
Highfields School

THE FOOTBALL

Football is the greatest sport,
You need no bats just a ball.
There are lots of teams like Derby and Wolves,
So come and play but you can win or lose.
Come and play you'll have a blast,
Players like Yorke who are really fast.
Come and play, you'll have a great time,
Loads of kits, even coloured lime.

Paul Chapman (12)
Highfields School

TELEPHONES

The secrets I've heard
Can never be told
My life is a never ending gossip
I've heard some lies
That could never be forgiven
So a secret I must keep 'em
I've heard the story from both sides
Know my family well
From love to hatred
I've know it all
Seen friends argue who never speak again
I've heard some sadness and some sorrow
But joy as well I've felt
I am that contact
That brings you together
I've always listened to what you have said.

Melanie Smith (13)
Highfields School

THE SPIDER

I've seen him
He's there
Creeping along the floor

He's made his web
Hiding in a corner
Trying to catch flies

He catches one
He sucks out the blood
Finished he wraps it up.

Victoria Marchant (13)
Highfields School

MAN ON THE MOOOON

One man wanted to be the first on the moon,
so he left on a cow with automatic zoom.
The cow jumped over the moon one night,
this really was quite a sight.
The man on the cow was hanging upside down,
admiring the view of his own home town.
But the cow jumped too far,
and they landed on a star.

The star started moving towards the sun,
this wasn't the old man's idea of fun.
So he jumped off using the cow as a kite,
they smashed straight into a satellite.
They bounced off it pretty quick,
which made the old man feel quite sick.

The man landed splat on the moon,
the cow went for Earth and got there quite soon.
The man got stuck on the moon forever,
which I really don't think was very clever.
If you ever think you can see him, you can
give a wave to the lonely old man!

Natalie Shooter (12)
Highfields School

ROBIN REDBREAST

Robin, robin redbreast,
Sitting on that tree,
Please sing a song just for me,
Then fly in the sky,
Then I can watch you,
Fly very high.

Cheryl Ward (11)
Highfields School

MY SISTER

My sister's only three
Though she thinks she's as old as me
She likes things to go her way
She screams and screams to have her say
She scribbles over my school books
Then gives me some awful looks
Though sometimes she is nice as pie
But then she will just cry and cry

She likes to play with all my stuff
The way she plays can be quite rough
Things off my desk disappear
Where they go I'll never hear

Sometimes she drives my mum spare
No wonder mum's getting grey hair
She makes my brother see only red
Then he says things that should not be said
She never lets me have a rest
She is a real little pest

But when I get cross
I tell her 'I'm the boss'
Then I shout 'Go away'
She just says 'Please let me stay'
Then she smiles her sweetest smile
I have to give in after a while
Though usually we get on really well
Me and my sister Isobelle.

Chlöe Newton (13)
Highfields School

CARS

Cars are built to get around
That is why they cost a lot of pounds
On a car you have a number plate
You can even have 1 MATE
Colours vary from blue to pink
When you choose you have to think
If you buy a BMW
It will never ever trouble you
If you buy a Mercedes Benz
You will find you have a lot of friends
If you want your speed much greater
Just step on the accelerator
If you want to win the race
You must then set the pace
If you hit the brake pedal
You will never win that gold medal
Do you hear my engine roar?
That is what I bought it for
When you are twenty-five
Do you think you'll be able to drive?

James Bance (13)
Highfields School

THE FOREST

The sun is gazing through the trees,
Casting a shadow below,
The darkness starts to fade away,
To reveal the midday sun.

The stomping of hooves,
The singing of birds,
The splashing of fish,
And the roar of the bear.

The grasses are swaying in the wind,
The sky is swarmed with migrating birds,
The water crashing into the gorge,
The forest woken by the sounds of the wild.

The night-time has come, like the circle of life,
The animals stop, scatter and sleep,
One animal wakes, flies with the wind,
This is the night dwellers' forest.

Cliff Fawcett (13)
Highfields School

STEELERS

The adrenaline pumps around the rink,
Players move fast and slink,
Slashing sticks and angry words,
The referee whistles like a vicious bird.

Darting, dashing, daring moves,
Body slams go with the groove,
Pom-pom dancers scream and shout,
There's a foul, the ref shouts 'Time out!'

The puck leaps long and fast,
The Steelers are putting on a charge at last,
It looks as if there's going to be a goal,
The players rush forward in a shoal.

The opposition look savage and 'ard,
The Steelers rush for the net they guard,
2 and 11 try in their time,
But the one who scores is number . . .
　　　　9 Priestlay.

Laura Donaldson (13)
Highfields School

THE BIG RUGBY MATCH

The players come out onto the pitch,
All the crowd yelling and shouting,
A whistle blows, the match starts,
The ball comes into action,
Crash, bang, wallop, the players collide,
Scrum down, line out, try, England have scored,
More tries come for England and Scotland,
The final whistle blows,
England fans erupt with cheers,
The players walk off the pitch,
England have won.

Ashley Statham (12)
Highfields School

SPACE

Space, it's a strange place.
It's all dark and black with lots of
Stars in the back.
Are there people up there?
Maybe one day they'll give us a scare.
They'll come down in the middle of the night,
I think it will give everyone quite a fright.
They might be green,
We'll all scream,
And maybe there'll be a war.
I don't think I like it after all.

Nicola Lloyd (12)
Highfields School

THE YEAR 2020

T wenty years since the millennium.
W ater's getting scarce.
O nly an inch of rain in the last month.

T hey say it's getting worse.
H ave you seen the latest TVs?
O ut in the shops yesterday.
U ltra sound.
S uper picture.
A nd all this is on your wrist!
N issan cars now have wings.
D riving's never been such fun.

A stronauts have spotted weird creatures on the moon.
N ow they're convincing us there really is life there.
D ial your friends and see them too.

T elephones now have visual screens.
W ars continue not all solved yet.
E ndless bombings in parts of the world.
N earer now to holidays in space.
T hey're building a hotel up there.
Y ears from now . . . who knows?

James Micallef (12)
Highfields School

OUR HOLIDAY IN FRANCE

We all pack the car,
It's all 'I'll give a hand.'
The ferry sets off,
We lose sight of our homeland.

Once in France,
The boiling sun comes out.
The journey's so long,
3000 miles, or there about.

We arrive in the mountains,
It's colder up here.
We ride in a cable car,
The ground's not so near!

After a week it's off to the Med',
The traffic jams drive you mad.
We set off home,
The weather gets bad.

We arrive back,
It's cold and wet.
But we'll return,
I bet!

Matthew Cannon (14)
Highfields School

CRICKET - THE LAST MAN

There I was coming in,
The last man.
A passing word of 'good luck' from the coach.
I finally get to the crease,
Feeling as good as new.
Then I realised,
No it couldn't be true,
Who was coming up to bowl?
No one else except the fastest bowler in the world.
Suddenly I didn't feel well,
My stomach started to churn,
I steadied my feet,
I steadied my bat.
That was it, no turning back.
Here he comes, fast like a rocket,
Then I saw through his disguise.
He was trying to trick me with his slower ball.
But!
He wasn't.
Straight on the middle stump.
I felt ashamed and embarrassed.
I tried to look up.
But I couldn't, so I hung my head low.
I still couldn't bat after all that practise.
But at least I'd had a go.

Karl Newton (12)
Highfields School

THE LAST PENALTY

The whistle blew
After extra-time
A discarded cup
Clattered across the area.

Several players slumped
Every second dragged
The pleasant sun
Heating my body
Cold with the fear of losing.

First John Smith hit the bar
Then their man went too far
Our man scored
And their forward roared
And the ball went wide and hit a car.

The next four went in past the keepers
It was down to Jeff Johnson
Tall but frozen he stood.

He ran up and hit the ball
It flew into the net
The crowd rose up with ecstatic applause
A better time you surely couldn't get.

Chris Hardy (12)
Highfields School

AUTUMN APPROACHES

A nip in the air,
Morning and night,
Autumn has come,
Breeze blows, the leaves fall to the ground,
Reds and golds, a lovely sight.
I look outside, it's going dark, only 8 o'clock at night.
Nights out, kids playing football, now they're saying
'Stay indoors.'
Watching TV and homework to be done,
I know I'll collect conkers when they're ready and ripe,
Thread through the string, crack I've lost, mine has split,
Bad choice of conker, I'll try again.
The leaves crackle from under my feet, it's getting chilly.
I know I'll go home, sit by the fire, get comfy in my chair,
Put the kettle on,
Then I'll know winter is on its way.

Sarah Hatch (13)
Highfields School

FARMING

I work on the farm all day
It's hard work with no pay
But day after day
The work won't go away
The cows go moo and moo all day
The chickens go cluck, cluck
And the sheep
Go bah bah, so all in all
It's not hard work but I like to
Play with the animals all day.

Jamie Wood (11)
Highfields School

FOOTBALL

22 legs upon a field,
Playing for the Charity Shield,
The game begins,
The fans all shout,
They know what it's all about!

Shearer has the goal in sight,
He won't give up without a fight,
A quick pass to Batty,
He takes a shot,
It flies over the penalty spot.

Now Derby are on the attack,
Biaino gives it a thumping whack,
The goalkeeper dives,
It hits the net,
How good is this game going to get?

Gregg Swift (11)
Highfields School

OUR SCHOOL

Highfields School, what a place,
In maths they're throwing round a pencil case.
In English they're talking and chatting galore,
In science they're experimenting and chatting some more.

Then there's the forms BC and ML,
These two give their teachers hell.
And then there's PH, a quieter form,
But even they cause quite a storm.

Next comes dinner, a busier time,
The dinner ladies try to sort out a line.
The year 10s push in, rude and a pain,
The year 9s move out, screaming in vain.

Now it's the end of a busy day,
The teachers are cheering and shouting 'Hurray.'
The pupils are running, but still miss their bus,
And then they cause the teachers more fuss.

Rachel Siddall (13)
Highfields School

YE OLD MAN

In the dismal looking city sits a right old codger,
With a feeble looking face and an overcast smile.
In his moth-eaten clothes and a glare within his eyes,
He sits there all night watching people passing by.
Throwing insults as if it's some game,
Looking out for people to take all the blame.
Ranting and raving his narrow minded ways,
Eating leftovers that've been out for days.
Tightly clasping his pint of old beer,
He rocks and sways, mumbling a cheer.
His hideous aroma filling the streets,
Putting off the people in which he meets.
Like a big of old washing neglected and torn,
Thrown out for no reason, just hasn't been worn.
Dark and dull he sits alone,
His previous lifestyle totally unknown.

Abby Hampson (13)
Highfields School

BABYSITTING

Babysitting is just for me,
For it's as easy as 1, 2, 3.
Ella is as good as gold,
And she does what she is told.

Ella likes her cuddly toys,
She laughs and giggles,
And makes a noise.
It really is quite entrancing,
To see her jumping, skipping,
And dancing.

I make her a bottle,
Before bed,
She likes to have
Stories read.
Her eyelids close,
As she is sleeping,
I hope she doesn't wake,
And starts weeping.

My job is nearly done,
Ella and I had lots of fun.
All is quiet now,
And I have to wait,
For mum to return.
I hope it won't be too late.

Nicola Morley (12)
Highfields School

YOUNG AND OLD

When all the world is young, lad,
And all the trees are green;
And every goose a swan, lad,
And every lass a queen;
Then hey for boot and horse, lad,
And round the world away;
Young blood must have its course, lad,
And every dog his day.

When all the world is old, lad,
And all the trees are brown;
And all the sport is stale, lad,
And all the wheels run down;
Creep home, and take your place there,
The spent and maimed among . . .
God grant you find one face there
You loved when all was young.

Sean Martin (11)
Highfields School

THE MAN FROM EALING

There was a young man from Ealing,
Who was fixing a hole in the ceiling,
He looked outside, squinted his eyes,
And fell out into West Ealing.

Then there was his mate on holiday in Spain,
Whose bum was in terrible pain, pain, pain,
He pulled down his pants, saw loads of ants,
Who sheltered inside from the rain, rain, rain.

Dean Kirkman (13)
Highfields School

THE CAT

The cat wakes from its sleep
and walks out onto the street
into the night's breeze.
It walks into a wood
and into a churchyard.

The cat stalks in the mist,
it will go into fearful places,
it is not afraid.
A mouse nibbles on a nut,
the cat sees it and jumps,
sudden death.

When day breaks it slinks into darkness,
like a ghost hiding from the sun,
then sleeps till the day is done.
Then as soon as night comes
it walks out into the moonlight.

Erin Cooper (12)
Highfields School

REVENGE

Revenge she sees,
Revenge she wants,
Revenge she craves,
Revenge she will get.

Every moment since that day,
He's lived in fear of this time,
But now the turn was his,
Questions he puts to her,
Answers he doesn't get.

She walked boldly into his life,
Afraid of not a thing,
He admired her strength,
And she knew what she
Wanted from him.

The sound of a gunshot whistled,
Bird chirps came as they flew in fear,
He looked away,
After everything he did not
Want to see.

Gemma Smedley (14)
Highfields School

MY BEDROOM

My bedroom is my hiding place
A place to slip away
From all the pressures of daily life
My refuge every day.

My bedroom is my reading room
A place to read my books
To slip into a dream place
Of kings and queens and crooks.

My bedroom is my childhood place
A place with all the toys
That bring back many memories
That bring back so much joy.

My bedroom is my favourite place
The place I love so much
A place to sleep and play and work
It hasn't lost its touch.

Megan Pyne (12)
Highfields School

FOOTBALL

Football is the greatest sport,
there's even a player called Stefan Schnoor.
Full of teams that are good and bad,
and when Man U win it makes me *mad!*
Football is the greatest sport,
there's loads of teams that fill the world.
Patrick Kluivert and Dwight Yorke,
even better than chips and pork.
Teams called Inter and Liverpool too,
I support Sheffield U, who do you?
So come on guys and watch a game,
and once you've seen it you won't be the same.

William Wragg (12)
Highfields School

EARTH

No one knows how our earth began.
Perhaps a dazzling meteor crashed and enveloped the sun.
What made that star home to the sun?
Maybe a myriad of dots were dancing around,
And magically transformed into a sound.
The sound drew dots to swirl and dance together,
To make an earth forever and ever.
Now we've discovered this beautiful place,
Let's begin the human race.

Jessica Heaton (12)
Highfields School

MONEY

Money is such a fantastic thing, it drives all people crazy,
most people worship money, driving them sincerely zany.
All people devote their lives to it, counting every penny,
that's why, as people say, which seems quite true to me,
money makes the world go round and round,
right round it should.
But money now and how it has been for quite a darn few years,
has changed the way we look around at everything we see.
Imagine a world with no such thing as money.
There would be no such thing as poor and people who steal money.
If there was a world with no such thing as money,
jealousy would be no cause of any kind of trouble.
Crimes, murders, robbery, theft would most certainly
be a thing of the past!

Chris Elliott (12)
Highfields School

FRANCE

River Saine runs through Rouen
Through Paris round Notre Dame
The Eiffel Tower's in Paris
That is a sight you must not miss.

The French Alps near River Rone
Stretch right up to River Saone
French baguettes and frogs' legs too
Find out which one's right for you.

Kathryn Mann (12)
Highfields School

My Amazing Car

I like driving in my car,
It does not go very far,
When I'm going extremely fast,
I sometimes see a snail crawl past.

My car is held together, only just,
By a load of orangey rust.

My car is not a brand new Porsche,
But it gets me south and north.

My car has only 3 rusty wheels and a door,
Because I am so very poor,
But when I start earning more,
I might buy another door.

Daniel Marchington (12)
Highfields School

A Little Green Man From Mars

Is the moon made of cheese?
Is Pluto illuminous yellow?
Is there a little green man from Mars?

Are there black holes that suck you in?
Has Saturn got a million rings?
Is there a little green man from Mars?

Would the sun melt me?
Has Jupiter a big black wart?
Is there a little green man from Mars?

Laura Dowsett (12)
Highfields School

AUTUMN

Red, yellow, gold, russet,
Brown, orange,
Are the colours to be found.

Under your feet where you tread,
Conkers, leaves and berries.

Crunchy, crispy, golden leaves,
Crunch and crisp,
When disturbed.

Everything hibernating,
Nicely in the trees.
It is the best season of all
It is *autumn*.

William Matthew Young (12)
Highfields School

SPIDER

What's that in the bath?
It can't be,
It is,
Do I dare?
I can't pick it up!
I must,
Here goes,
Ahhhh!

Alice Vale (11)
Highfields School

SPACE LANDS

The galaxy is full of stars
The solar system is full of planets
And the sun
A burning mass of gas and fire
Burning brightly
With its powerful rays
Shining in straight lines
The moon, its reflection
And all the tiny little stars
Are bright and chirpy
Even on a cloudy night
And each one individually
Has its own perfect shape and size
Plough and Great Bear are beautiful star shapes
Floating in the atmosphere
No air, no gravity
The sky is alive with silver dots
Gold and yellow
Glowing against the dark, deep, everlasting sky
All alone with nothing but the moon
Reflecting the sun
White and lumpy with craters the size of houses
A big white ball
Glowing with the stars against the dark and
Everlasting sky.

Karis Hodgkinson (13)
Highfields School

LIFE!

Life is for living
Life can be enjoyable
Life is sometimes fast and exciting
It can take you wherever you want to go

Life is for living
Life is love and sometimes hate
Life is heaven and hell
Life is up and then it is down
But life is still always around.

Tom Wright (11)
Highfields School

THE RIGHT FORMULA

All lined up on the grid
preparing themselves for the start.
with the revving, roaring of the engines
the tension mounts.
Red turns to green, the driver's zoom off.
Each driver has a rival he must beat.
Blurred colours whizzing past, rain or shine.
The noise is immense.
All the drivers are under a lot of pressure,
Faster! Faster! Faster!
The flag waves at a back marker.
It's fast, frantic, furious action,
the brake disks glow at a corner
his foot hits the accelerator.
Beads of sweat drip down his face.
Two laps till the chequered flag.
Heart-beat pounding, pounding!
Coming up to the last corner, he sees the line
and zooms past in flying colours
to take the chequered flag and win the Grand Prix.
His entire team is jumping for joy,
the driver is ecstatic, but relieved
until the next time!

Adam Taylor (11)
Highfields School

THE SUMMER HOLIDAYS

The summer holidays have already past
We didn't think that they would last.
Warmer weather we pray to come soon
Longer, brighter nights, we see less of the moon
Jetting off to somewhere sunny
With lots and lots of your money.
Sun, sea and golden sand
More than likely in a different land.
Buckets and spades are fun on the beach.
Time for a chocolate ice-cream each.
Roses blooming with bright flowers.
No more of those April showers.
Feet sinking into soft, warm sand.
On a sunny day in the park near the band.
Summer holidays are lots of fun
Even though it gets hot in the sun.
How I love holiday time
Especially when the weather is fine.

Lucie Needham (12)
Highfields School

KALEIDOSCOPE COLOURS

Look into the kaleidoscope
What do you see?
Red, yellow, green and blue
All of them fluent colours
Must *resemble* you
I must be dreaming or maybe *not*
All of them fluent colours
They all resemble you.

Alex Barker (13)
Highfields School

THE SCHOOL AT NIGHT

When all the teachers have gone away,
The caretaker's work is done for the day.
The school becomes a lonely place,
Dark and silent, not a face.

Shadows cast by the teacher's chair,
No coats or bags, the cloakroom's bare.
There's no stampede on the corridor floor,
No scraping of chairs, not a knock on the door.

No footballs flying around the playground,
Just dry leaves fluttering, the only sound.
Until the darkness of night has passed away,
When children arrive to start a new day.

Tom Harvey (13)
Highfields School

KALEIDOSCOPE

Look inside a kaleidoscope, a world of
shape and colour,
Bold and bright,
Forming beautiful patterns,
A world of hope and pleasure.

Look inside a kaleidoscope, a mind of
creation and themes,
Creative pictures,
With different meanings,
A mind of wishes and dreams.

Look inside a kaleidoscope.

Kirsten Hill (13)
Highfields School

MITTENS

A yawn, a stretch, sleepy-head,
Sitting comfy on my bed,
A call, a shout, his name is cried,
The lazy feline wanders by,
Into our garden he goes to play,
Whether the sky is blue or grey,
Prancing, prowling, sneaking around,
Sniffing the air - listening for sound,
A rustle, a squeak, a whining cry,
Foiled now - the urge to pry,
Tired and bored of this game,
Time for sleep as he hears his name.

Suzanne Lilley (13)
Highfields School

THE FIRST DAY OF WINTER

The first day of winter
The snow was falling from the clouds
They were white and fluffy and as thick as they seemed
On the hills like it would only last one day
The road was empty, there were no cars
The shops were closed from the snow
People are not to be seen
The houses are thick like ice-cream
The doors were shut, the windows are closed
The snow was nearly over, everybody knows
The children are crying out for it to stay
But the mums all say 'Hip, hip, hooray!'

Cameron Freestone (13)
Highfields School

THE UNWANTED GUEST

Dark clouds lumber overhead like a funeral march,
Its features reflect onto faces dark, dull, dismal, harsh.
Then he arrives like an unwanted guest,
Spit, spot, drip, drop.
From inside all you can hear is his message,
Tip-tap, pitter-patter.
The clouds start to groan,
And people moan.
Screwed up faces, squinting eyes,
Curling shoulders, looking to the sky.
A dark shadow creeps over the streets,
Feet begin to scurry tapping his beats.
The unwanted guest barges in,
He makes sure you know he's arrived.

Umbrellas open out, raincoats, wellies pulled on,
Their colours lighting up the sky.
You still cannot hide even inside.
You can hear his message, tapping, rapping,
Drumming on the roof and windows,
Pipes gushing, puddles, splashing.
Streets are almost empty,
Hiding from the visitor.
His icy hands stabbing your skin,
His feet start stamping on your head.
His friend drifts him across the land,
Over grass, sea water and sand.
Umbrellas slowly go down,
The sun starts to peep out.
Doors are safely locked,
He cannot come back even if he knocked.

Sally Maddocks (13)
Highfields School

A STORM

It was cold and wet
and raining hard.
The wind grew louder
and whistled.
The sky rumbled and became grey.
The rain started belting on the ground.
The trees were swaying side to side.
The branches near my window scratched
and tapped. I crawled down in my bed
trying to get those sounds out of my head.
The gate slammed shut. It made me jump
I got lower and lower in my bed.
Trying and trying again to get those
sounds out of my head.
The rain became lighter
the wind became a breeze
I fell fast asleep.

Carla Thompson   (11)
Highfields School

MY FAMILY

My mum looks like an alien,
with a great big wart on her nose.
My sister looks like a gremlin,
with smelly, sticky toes.
My dad looks like an old toad,
and is rather sneaky.
My brother looks like a gorilla,
and is really freaky!
And as for me, well . . .
I look like all of 'em!

Amy Thomas (12)
Highfields School

LULLABY BIRDSONG

I open my window to hear
the gentle lull of birdsong.
Whistling on the wind,
Soft and smooth,
High and flowing,
Never-ending,
Like the agile movement of the birds.
From brambles to bushes,
Hollows to hedgerows,
In and out of their secure little nests;
Until the lullaby slowly grows fainter and fainter
As I close my window;
Until the soothing sound has gone.

Kirsty McNaught (13)
Highfields School

ANIMALS LOCKED UP

Animals are locked up
Put in a cage all shut up
Dark all day, dark all night
See no day, see no light.

What a fright this must be, to have no food or drink to see
Dark through day, dark through night
One day maybe you'll see the light.

Able to reach for freedom - start new life
Now you are free and it is light
Light all day, light all night
Now you are able to see clear light.

Samantha Brassington (13)
Highfields School

THE END

She stands on the cliff
She cries - tears stream down her face
She clings to the air around her
She doesn't want it to end.

But it's been going on too long
The feeling of being trapped has never left her
All her life there has been no escape
This is her only way.

She always loved the cliffs
This is the only place it can end
Up here there's no one to hurt her
If only she thinks

With one hand she wipes away the tears
She sniffs and whimpers like a child
In the distance a man watches her
He knows that the time has come.

She takes a step towards the edge
She fills her lungs with cool air
She peers down, whimpers,
Closes her eyes and plunges into the water.

She no longer feels the pain
She feels numb and free
She's escaped from the cruel world above
He can't hurt her anymore.

Katie Boitoult (13)
Highfields School

AUTUMN

The spring sounds fall away
Hidden beneath the new
Autumn's arrived
The leaves turn bright, light colours
The birdsong quietens down.
The hedgehog goes into hibernation
Deep beneath the real world
Trees go bare
The forest is still, quiet
Except for the sound of
Trickling water
A breeze blows gently
Clouds start to move overhead
Dark, grey, menacing
The rain starts to fall
Scuttling sounds, running around.
Thunder claps, splitting the eerie silence.

Patricia Clark (11)
Highfields School

MY BEDROOM

M y bedroom is my favourite place
Y our bedroom is probably yours.

B ecause it is quiet and I can do my own thing
E very thing is in the right place
D ivided in two, the
R ight of the room is for fun and I
O ften invite my friends there
O r the left side is for sleeping
M y bedroom is my favourite place.

Sophie Carnell (12)
Highfields School

UNTITLED

Oh! How I wish that I could read
Everyone else can
But oh not me!
I don't think I'm daft
I know I'm not thick
I try and I try but it just won't
Click!
Problems with spelling
Problems with maths.
Which is the way?
Where is the path?
Who do I tell?
Who do I ask?
Won't someone help me
To achieve these tasks?

Matthew Stokes (11)
Highfields School

ASHLEY DAVIS

A   shley Davis
S   hares his things
H   as lots of fun as well.
L   oves to play football
E   ven likes his sister
Y   ou're weird his friends say to him.

D   ays go by but never bad
A   shley collects cars
V   auxhall his worst
I   ncredible collection his friends say
S   ometimes he goes to the Motor Show.

Ashley Davis (12)
Highfields School

THE TELEPHONE

A telephone is a wonderful thing
But that's until it starts to ring
Then we all shout 'Not again!'
That phone really is a pain.
And if we don't answer it quick
The answer machine goes click
And then my mum's voice starts to drone
About there being no one home.
It starts to ring when we're having tea
I wouldn't mind so much if it was for me
But it's nearly always for my dad
And that's what really makes me mad
Because then we have to keep the noise down
Or my dad starts to frown
Once it starts it doesn't stop
Until my dad's head is about to pop.
I like to chat to my mates
After six is the cheap rate
Like the advert says it's good to talk
But sometimes I'd rather take a walk.
Then we all go out for the day
Somewhere peaceful far away
Suddenly my ears start to pound
I can hear a funny sound.
It sounds just like my dad's mobile.
He promised he'd turn it off for a while
It's an ice-cream van up the street
It looks like we're all in for a treat.

Nicky Marples (11)
Highfields School

THE PAIN OF MY LIFE

Crushed like a snail
My heart is broken in two.

Played with like a doll
My heart is broken in four.

Treated as if I'm not there
My heart is broken in eight.

Hurt like a bruise
My heart is broken into a thousand pieces.

Pain like I've never experienced before
I can no longer count the pieces of my heart.

Stabbed as an arrow rips through my heart
My heart cannot go on anymore.

Melissa Goodall (12)
Highfields School

MY HAMSTER

My hamster's got little beady eyes
Four paws and a nose that is pink.
She's fluffy because she's covered in fur
And is cuter than a nasty big mink.

She lives in a cage in my bedroom
And keeps me awake through the night.
By spinning her exercise wheel
And squeaking and squeaking in fright.

Catherine Allen (11)
Highfields School

MANCHESTER UNITED

Manchester United are the best
Better than the rest
Never lose a game
Never in shame.

Always score a goal
Usually Andy Cole
When the goalie scores
He always gets applause.

Signed Dwight Yorke
With a leg like a fork
When Scholes is in space
United win the race.

Gregory Smith (11)
Highfields School

FOOTBALL, FOOTBALL

Football, football is a game
to score a goal is the aim.
Football, football we shout and cheer
when our team starts to appear.
Football, football the whistle blows
soon there has been several goals.
Football, football a tackle is made
we put the other team in the shade.
Football, football the time is up
We are the champions
We've won the cup.

Andrew Swift (11)
Highfields School

YOU AND I

I cannot hurt a spider
I cannot kill a fly
The animals and insects are here
Like you and I.

Some animals live in cages some
Animals starve and die but all
Should be cared for just like you and I.

I like dogs and cats and rabbits
I could not tell you why
But I know they need a
Friend the same as you and I.

Kathryn Gregory (11)
Highfields School

THE STORM

It was ice-cold
The wind was blowing strongly.
The waves were roaring.
Sand was blowing everywhere
then suddenly everything went quiet.
The wind was whistling softly
Seagulls flew into mid air
and then all you could hear was the
call of the seagulls and the swiftness
of the air.

Hannah Nadin (11)
Highfields School

CASTLES IN THE TIDE

In the heat of the sun
making castles in the sand
with the waves lapping
on the shore.
As the day goes by the
sunset comes down
and the waves wash the
castles away beneath the
cool glimmering sea.

Gwenny Robson (11)
Highfields School

MY PET DOG

I have a pet dog called Holly.
She was from a rescue centre.
When we first saw her she was skinny.
You could see her ribs
The only way she could hurt you
is to lick you to death.
She's black and white and looks
like a puppy.

Chloe Bond (11)
Highfields School

LOVE

L ove is one of the nicest words you will ever read or hear
O h how I wish the thing I love would love me back too
V alentine is its name, quite appropriate I think
E ven though it's just a teddy bear.

Ann Hawley (11)
Highfields School

A TREAT TO EAT

A treat to eat is a nice lamb chop
nice, juicy and fresh.
My master always says to me
'Oh you do get in a mess!'
Every night I go to bed
I have a nice dream
and this time I dreamt that
the world was made of ice-cream!
In the morning my master wakes up
he comes down stairs and says
'Who's been a good pup!'
When I go for a walk in the long long grass,
my master always watches out for sharp and pointy glass.

Joel Stackhouse (11)
Highfields School

THE SEAL PUP

Seal pup fluffy and white
Wet rocks reflecting your light
Safe by your mother's side
Below evening skies
Then into the water you glide.

Seal pup swimming with grace
Slipping from place to place
Jumping up to the dock
Filling yourself with shock
Then swimming back to your rock.

Robert O'Connor
Highfields School

IMAGINE!

Is the sky just black,
Or is it liquorice or flap jack?

Are the stars just blobs,
Or are they milk or bottle tops?

Are the tree roots just black dark branches,
Or are they string wrapped round your ankles?

Is your bed just a place to rest,
Or is it a warm bird's nest?

Laura Gillie (11)
Highfields School

ITCHES

That itch I had on my back last night
the one which wouldn't go away.
I rubbed and scratched it
but still it wouldn't go away.
When I went to the fish and chip shop
it haunted me and made my chips go flying.
So if you have an itch
let me tell you what to do
Beware!

Zoe Urquhart (11)
Highfields School

THE STAR THAT WOULD NOT GLEAM

One gentle night, I had a dream
About a star that would not gleam.
It lay in the sky not saying a word
In the star's mind *to twinkle* would not have occurred.
All the rest of the stars were gleaming like gold
But this star was pale white, lonesome and cold.

The other stars began teasing around.
The gleam-less star was unhappy and frowned.
Nobody loved him, nobody cared
Even though the star knew that he shared.
He was getting so tiresome of being left out
'Why do you not like me?' he started to shout.

The gleaming stars just laughed and played on
'You're nothing at all but a little con.'
The star wept and cried about what they said
He agreed with the others and wished he was dead.
He closed his eyes and would not speak
He fell very ill and became very weak.

A powerful voice called out from afar
'Why do they scorn you, why do they mar?'
All the star did was cry and weep.
'I'm nothing at all, my gleam I can't keep.'
He carried on weeping in a pitiful way
And no other word he wanted to say.

The voice told a story of sorrow and love
'My dear sweet star, just picture a dove.
Elegant, playful with peace in its glide,
These are the things you have hidden inside.
No matter how hurtful a harsh word can seem,
Within your soul, you will always gleam.'

William Parkinson (11)
Highfields School

THE VAMPIRE

The part leader of the vampire race
Awakes thirsty for blood
He evokes his memory
Of that one big flood.

His eyes are evil and diabolical
His hands are red as hell.
His skin is pale and white like snow
The hour strikes one on the bell.

He mutters does that evil doer
He is very covetous for blood.
So he picks on an ewe
No chance of evading - quite amazing.

Groups of trick or treaters
Are walking home at night.
Prepared to take no pity
He takes another bite.

The vampire swoops down
This to be his last.
A boy grabs a stick
And penetrates his heart.

The vampire now dying
The boy ran back home
And then with thoughts of violence
He wakes and utters . . . blood!

Tom Stanton (12)
Highfields School

TREE

It lives and stands still as iron
but occasionally twists and turns.
Its limbs always climb up and keep growing.
And in autumn they singe and they burn.

In summer it's bursting with colour.
It wears its green coat with pride.
The tree looks joyful and happy,
like its feelings are nothing to hide.

In autumn it looks like it's angry
its leaves have now turned golden red.
Its limbs now are heavily laden
Its fruit taken by farmers - nothing said.

Mid autumn/ mid winter it shivers
as its gown is now all stripped away.
But it still stands as if nothing's happened
just resting, just sleeping today.

In winter it gets covered in snow
and now it's completely bare.
Its arms are distinctive and twig-like
but the tree stands, it will always be there.

Angelina Shiers (12)
Highfields School

MY FAMILY

My mum is summer in a beautiful garden
My dad is thunder at a football match
My sister is laughter on even a rainy day.

Katharine Inglis (11)
Highfields School

STAR DOME

As you go down the pitch-black tunnel
It's like you're going down a giant funnel.
As you enter the dome.
The music that's playing makes you feel at home.
As you see the stars moving around you
It really starts to enthral you.
It makes you feel as if you're moving into another world.
The stars around you begin to whirl.
As you look at the stars above
It feels as if you're flying like a dove.
As the stars start to disappear
You realise that you're back here.

Thomas Baston (13)
John Flamsteed Community School

ALONE ON MY OWN

Alone on my own, the night is drawing closer now
it's cold and dark, I'm scared.
Alone on my own, standing on the platform station
I wish my mum was here.
My mum now she's gone, I may never see her again.
I'll miss her plump red podgy face and how she made
me feel so safe.
Alone on my own, I am getting weary now but
I must stay awake as the train should be
here soon to take me away from this place.
So I may never return again.

Sarah Thomas (14)
John Flamsteed Community School

THE MARS ROBOT

The robot landed
There was tension at the space station
The first pictures were transmitted
There was a gasp!
The robot moved slowly, silently, across
the rocky wasteland.
No sign of life.
The communications were breaking up
A fuzzy noise was beginning to sound.
First the sound broke up
Then the transmission failed.
'Get it back on line,' shouted the commander.
Then there was a noise
Coming from the robot
The picture came on line
A bright green face appeared.
It was a species unknown to man
The transmission broke up again
We have found life on Mars.

Sam Scaife (13)
John Flamsteed Community School

THE EXPERIMENT

Hubble dubble, toil and trouble,
Carbon burn and acid bubble,
Test tube shaking in the rack,
Beakers breaking with a crack.

Bunsen burners roaring high,
Student working out the 'Pi'
New solution being created,
'Is it acid or alkali rated?'

'I'll put a spatula of iron in,'
Broken beaker in the bin,
The solution bubbled violently,
And test tubes shook so silently.

Student wondered what to do,
Very quickly he then drew
Something that would conjure up . . .
Oh dear, the room blew up.

Grant Birkin (13)
John Flamsteed Community School

RUFUGEE

I've been on the run since last May.
Each night I pray it will end one day.
My family, my friends we're all in pain.
What's the point of war?
What will they gain?

We once made a living, we had a farm.
Our life was quite happy,
Thought we'd come to no harm.
But now we're hungry, starved and sad,
I love to dream of the life we once had.

My best friend Hakeem starved to death.
Last night I saw him take his last breath.

My sister Larna, she's only five
But we don't know if she's dead or alive.

Rachel Spink (12)
John Flamsteed Community School

THE EVACUATION POEM

On the train arriving there
The stopping noise gave me a scare.
Who would my new family be
Or would they even like me?

I miss my mum and dad that's true
And it's no secret either
I am so sad. Oh! What to do?
The sadness made me quiver.

I walked my fellow evacuees
Up the garden lane.
Past the tall and spooky trees
Never see mum again.

Ring, ring, ring the doorbell goes
Smarten up my fellows.
Tidy up and blow your noses
'Hello!' Tom's voice bellows.

'Will you take him?' she said to Tom.
My coat all covered in fur.
Battered, bruised and all gone wrong
'My name is William sir!'

You're as skinny as an ice-cream cone
Thought Tom when we first met.
Finally now I have a home
I bowed my head and slept.

James Leneve-Roff (13)
John Flamsteed Community School

NEVER DO I EVER

I was sitting on my bed
One day in August,
When I heard my mummy say to me
'My dear, I am so sorry
But you have to go
It's evacuation to the country.'

I knew well what it meant,
And I have to say
I've never been so scared in all my life.
I went to pack my bag
And gather all my things
I don't think I could cause my mum more strife.

We went down to the train
And as I climbed aboard,
My mummy turned and looked into my eyes.
'I promise you, my dear
That one day you'll be back
And never do I ever tell a lie.'

And then the whistle went
And as the train chugged on,
I saw my home city for the last time.
I sat with some old friends,
Everyone was quiet,
And then I knew our lives had become prime.

The war lasted five years;
And I did not forget,
A single day that passed as time went by.
I saw my mum at home.
She looked into my eyes
'And never do I ever tell a lie.'

Daisy Julian (13)
John Flamsteed Community School

TORTURE

Once again, no control over my body, it was torn in all directions as the invisible streaks of lightning took over my trembling body.

The cold, hard, wet floor hit me, like the hag's boot, then pain ricocheting through all that I can feel.

Can't fight anymore - just a puppet handled by a mad puppeteer, ruthless in his quest for knowledge. Death beckons, but is pushed away.

So much pain and the epileptic terror, caused by so little effort. I can see my naked feet as if they were a thousand miles off, splayed out at impossible angles.

The charged water, waves of pain. But the waves have not flooded my mind, it remains clear. A desert island, a calm in the storm of relentless pain and fear, with one thought - Isa.

Shelley Frith (15)
John Flamsteed Community School

REFUGEES

Refugees are people
People who are stranded
Stranded with no home and little food
Waiting for war and conflict to stop
Scared of bombs and gunshots
Scared of war
Normal people, sometimes not poor people
Who walk the streets day and night begging other
People for food and a place to live
Young children who rely on themselves
Searching for relatives and friends
Travelling miles and miles to find people.

Joe Bryan (13)
John Flamsteed Community School

PUPPET ON A STRING

I am dragged in late,
To dance and sing,
To watch the sparks of white and blue,
A puppet on a string.

I used to dance to a merry tune,
But now I follow a different beat,
Chained to the wall, and beaten raw,
A puppet on a string.

I used to laugh,
But now I cry,
As the torturer gives a sigh,
A puppet on a string.

I was once warm,
But now I'm cold,
As the blue white light crackles on,
A puppet on a string.

Now at home,
I laugh out loud,
I kept my secret safe inside,
This puppet disobeyed his strings!

James Gill (14)
John Flamsteed Community School

POEMS ON TORTURE
(Resources From Chapter 6 & 7)

Questioning, constantly,
Force beyond control.
Tell the truth
or torture and doom.
Voices speaking in total dark
My time has come
My time has come.
Blue and white lightning
was all I could see.
I'm doomed
I'll never be free
I'm innocent - I'm good.
I've followed all the rules I should
Instead I'm a puppet.
A beaten, swollen, half-conscious puppet.
The door opened,
I could be free! I could be free!
That's wishful thinking?
They've not finished with me.
Though writhing with pain
So bruised, and so sore
My mind it remains focused!
They'll hurt me no more!
Once away from *the house of laughter*
My testimony I'll shout
I'll no longer be *talking in whispers!*

Thomas Leighton (14)
John Flamsteed Community School

HE

He sits in the corner
And everyone stares,
Although they're all looking
Not one of them cares.
He pulls on his blanket,
Up tight round his ears,
To hold back the cold
To hold back his tears.
All he has now
Are the clothes on his back
All torn and dirty
All made from a sack
He sleeps in the gutter
He sleeps in the snow
If you lived like this
Wouldn't you like to know?
Where did you come from?
Where will you go?
How did you manage
To get so low?
Have you ever considered
As you walk down his street
To enter his world
When his eyes yours do meet
Don't be misguided,
Please make him a friend,
For one of these days
His suffering surely must end.

Holly Steel (15)
John Flamsteed Community School

THE SUN

A huge burning sizzling ball of fire,
snuggled up in the soft fluffy clouds.
Never moves, never makes a sound.
Suspended in space, it looks down on Earth, on us,
On small children drawing pictures
of the happy yellow suns in the sky.
From down below the sun looks warm and comforting
but up close it's an evil, angry, blazing, scorching monster.
It steams and smokes and boils with anger all day long.
The bad-tempered monster just sits there,
and stares at the world, at real life and real fun,
The sun has nothing.
The smouldering beast has lived nearly two
billion years.
Will it be here forever?
Nobody knows.
One day it will get so bored, so agitated, so mad
it will explode with anger
and burn itself out. Gone forever.
But if the sun goes, so do we.
For we can't live without the sun.

Jessica Holt (13)
Lady Manners School

THE RIVER

The river is a ferocious snake,
Its razor-sharp teeth slash the rocks to smithereens.
Its winding body swirls, sweeps, swishes,
Eroding the valleys on its long tireless journey.

Fish jump from its magical body,
And people gaze at its might and strength.
Whilst moaning trees weep in its waters,
Curious cows gape at the splendour.

Summer's like a parasite,
Sucking the river dry under the savage, vicious sun.
Whereas charitable autumn is caring,
Its plentiful downpours revitalise the reptile.

When the serpent reaches the end of its voyage,
It is conquered and destroyed, swallowed up and never to be seen again.
It becomes worthless and anonymous,
But ready to face a whole new adventure.

John Wright (13)
Lady Manners School

I LOVE YOU

I can talk about nothing,
yet mean everything,
when I speak to you.

The words I need,
I cannot find,
to tell you how I feel.
But you understand me.
You know what I mean
and what I want to say.

Do you feel the same,
when I say those words,
as I feel when you say them too?

I can talk about nothing,
yet mean everything,
when I speak to you.

I love you.

Vicky Crewe (13)
Lady Manners School

THE COLOUR OF YELLOW

Yellow is a colour,
like red, blue and green.
Because it is a colour,
it can be seen.

Yellow is a vastness,
the vastness of the air.
It is safe yet open,
with no obtrusive glare.

Yellow is an object,
the object of the land.
Not too huge, nor too feeble,
it is not overly grand.

Yellow is a power,
the power of the sun.
It is still and bold,
the power that kills none.

Yellow.

David Woods (13)
Lady Manners School

MUM

This is a poem about my mummy,
It's not very good, in fact it's crummy.
She is pretty thin, and not very tall
But very artistic when decorating the hall.

She is the secretary, at the junior school,
And all the kids think she's really cool.
She can't cook to save her life,
But Dad says she's a very good wife.

She feeds the cats and walks the dogs
And also tries to make bread cobs.
But lucky for us, she doesn't succeed
When the day's done, she loves to read.

She makes you laugh when you're down,
I think I should give my mum a crown.
I just want to say, 'I love you Mum.
Even after all the times you've smacked my bum!'

Eleanor Haskey (13)
Lady Manners School

SUMMER ENDS

Lying in the long, long grass
The seasons begin to change
The wind brings a chill to me
Nature starts to arrange
When it comes around again
It'll never be the same.

Peace is in the summer
Now sorrow spreads its wings
Autumn sets in today
Winter is too near
Misery conquers happiness
Until another year.

Lying in the long, long grass
Clouds are drifting by
As I think what will come tomorrow
Plants begin to die
Dreaming in this lost domain
Which you'll never see again.

Jonathan Buchanan (14)
Lady Manners School

INSOMNIA

Sleepless nights,
staring into darkness,
for hours on end.
Night after night
lying awake
in the shadows.
Aware of every sound,
every movement.

The moon is shining
through the curtains.
Cruising through the clouds.
Casting mysterious
shadows on the walls.

Uncontrollable imagination,
frightened by the creaks
of the floorboards,
the house settling.
Rain tapping on the windows.
Unexpected sounds.
In a silent, sleeping household.
Longing sleep.

Helen Yates (13)
Lady Manners School

THE STREET LAMP

When all is dark,
he wakes up yawning.
With a soft glow
he begins to shine.

He searches slowly,
growling,
sniffing.
Hunting for his prey.

Through the hours,
he whines and twists,
and then,
was that a glimpse of life?

It was.
It was.
He cries for joy,
for there is his victim.

As the prey walks past,
he shines upon it
and captures it
in his big, strong arms.

Then he lets it go,
as the sun starts to rise.
For it's time to rest,
until tomorrow night.

Charlotte Louise Hibbert (13)
Lady Manners School

THE MAD DASH FOR THE BUS

The bell goes and everyone cheers.
The mad dash for the bus.
The teachers inside
say, 'Be quiet.
Hush, hush, hush.'

Children here, children there.
The mad dash near the bus.
The patrol ladies
slow the crowds
and the drivers prepare for the rush!

People shout, others sing.
The mad dash on the bus.
The experienced driver
turns away,
and the engine goes, *whoosh!*

The noise decreases and quietens down.
The mad dash not on the bus.
Members of the public
jump on board.
At the front sits old Angus!

The bus stops at the end of the street.
The mad dash off the bus.
Parents wait
for their loved ones.
What a load of unwanted fuss!

James Duncan (13)
Lady Manners School

YOU ARE THE AXIS

You are the axis,
that my world spins on.
Without you my world has
no meaning.
It is a ball that appears solid
but locked away beneath the crust.
All my secrets and feelings are
melting down into liquid formation,
waiting for their chance of freedom.
A tiny lie or deceit could cause
a crack that would change everything.
All my emotions would bring disaster
and I would rapidly demolish all
the trust and respect I have ever
worked for.
So let this be a lesson to you,
nothing is as stable as it's made
out to be.
So never judge a book by its cover
or a human being by their
first impression .

Anna Laing (13)
Lady Manners School

THE BUTTERFLY

The butterfly does flutter by,
Among the soft green leaves,
Gracefully it flutters by,
In the summer's breeze.

The butterfly has pretty wings,
All in different colours,
On its flight to us it brings,
A gift of many wonders.

The butterfly can swoop and sway,
And feeds upon a flower,
Forget just what the Spice Girls say,
Remember *butterfly power!*

Jo Esders (13)
Lady Manners School

LAUGHTER

A loud cry of happiness pierces the room,
contagious, like fire spreading,
warming you all over.
Their eyes sparkle, their faces light up,
erupting like a volcano the warm lava
seeps through the air,
a comfort, a diversion.
They throw their heads back,
full of cheer and joy.
Faces crumple
as they laugh, laugh, laugh!

Lauren Thompson (13)
Lady Manners School

THE FLIGHT OF THE OWL

At night it takes flight through the misty sky,
dodging and diving through trees,
and then up like a thrust of wind.

        As the moon beams down on the deserted city,
           the owl hunts and stalks for its prey,
        like a shark in water his sharp eye spots his lunch.

Quickly but silently he swoops down,
in one attempt he traps it like a fish in a bowl.
It has no way out and in one mouthful it's gone.

        As he feeds on his catch he hears the sound of early risers,
           then one by one the street lights turn on,
        as if an alarm clock, telling the owl to set back.

At first a peaceful flight with only the noise of small birds,
the feel of the thick morning mist
and the bitter taste of dew.

        Then from out of the mist and into the trees the owl soars,
           but then a bang and a quiet whistle,
        as small pieces of metal fly through the air.

In a state of shock the owl delicately manoeuvres
amongst the trees.
Soaring and sailing through the mist as the noise becomes quieter
and then back to its home just as the morning sun rises.

Andrew O'Gorman (13)
Lady Manners School

BALLROOM DANCERS OF AUTUMN

How elegant they look in their gowns of green and suits of gold and
russet.
Each balletic figure, incandescent, emitting poise, grace and etiquette.
The band strikes up, the wind instruments whistle their tune.
The dancers are away, casting silhouettes in the light of the moon.
See them twist and turn in all their splendour.
See them float and fly and soar.
Emerald and amber against the diamond studded sky,
So beautiful and exquisite no amount of money can buy.
Yet it's a beauty which can be shared by all,
but only once a year, in the fall.
The dancers curl and bend,
before they come to their end.
On the evergreen carpet of the dance floor,
but they're not yet done, for we cry, 'Encore.'

Hannah Chapman (14)
Lady Manners School

THE RIVER

The river twists, turns and tangles through the night,
crashing and bashing against the weakening bank.
In a flash it collapses.
In a moment it's gone.
The town sleeps on oblivious to the destruction nearby.
When the day breaks it is all revealed,
or at least what is left of it.

What once was a river is now a lake.
The water is silent,
like the silence of an owl in flight, at night.
People are glaring, gazing and staring,
at the place where the barn once stood.
They look at the ground where the stables once were.
They sigh and they grieve,
for they know, that next year it will all happen again.
The river!

Tom Thurston (13)
Lady Manners School

THE WIND

Howling, screaming the beast rises from
the depths of time to strike a cold
chill into the land.
His moaning can be heard through windows
and doors, around rooftops in villages and cities.
His great paws crush trees and houses alike
when he strides around the sky.
Hearing the cries of many below he turns
a blind eye and carries on his duty of destruction.
Bound forever to walk the land and sky
raining havoc on mankind and changing the
landscape of time.
Then suddenly he stops, tired and bored
and crawls back to his lowly hole
ready to strike again at any moment.
Waiting, watching, ready and yet so still and
calm, at times a beast to mankind.
He can be a vicious monster or a gentle dove,
happily playing with the trees
but it depends on what mood he is in.

Philip Wride (14)
Lady Manners School

THE SEA

The sea is a fierce dragon,
green and full of motion.
Scraping his razor claws,
tearing the rock face,
swiping his victims down into the sea.
But when the sea is still and nothing moves,
the dragon sleeps . . . snooze, snooze, snooze.
Then later when the tide is in;
he's back to life
dark and grim.
His rolling eyes, his threatening paws,
pounding the beach; till bedtime calls.
And when all the tourists are lying there,
so still, relaxed, not a care in the world,
the huge dark dragon wakes again.
Plunging and diving he takes no prisoners.
Then later at night when the tide does go in,
he'll sleep until later, when needed again.

Stephen Pilcher (13)
Lady Manners School

ANGER

She lit the stove,
she felt something stir deep within.
Slowly, it set in, the realisation.
Could he really have done this to her?
She wouldn't, couldn't stop this anger rise,
was frightened by the way she began to despise.
She wanted to scream, 'Don't do this to me!'
As the temperature rose yet another degree.
Energy flowed, her soul simmered with heat,
steaming,
bubbling,
ready to explode.
She screamed to release the unbearable tension
as a piercing whistle shrilled in unison.
Both she and the water in the kettle
reached boiling point.

Laura Haigh (13)
Lady Manners School

THE BEACH

She walks along, the warm sand pressing against the soles of her feet.
The sea air blowing against her hair.
The water lapping against her feet,
like a puppy, licking her affectionately.
A crab scuttles by,
not afraid,
barely noticing her.
She is an imposer upon them,
but they bear her no grief.
She carries on,
the sea so gently swaying,
in time, it will become a monster,
a fierce growling beast,
smashing against he rocks,
tearing at the seabed
but now, daytime so calm.
The sky's blue
there is no wind.
The sea almost like a clock,
ever-changing as the day goes on.

Felicia Nicol (13)
Lady Manners School

THE WATERFALL

It's deafeningly peaceful,
From a distance it's a rainbow of light,
Colourful against the glowing sun.
Lower, to where it hits the river,
It is violent,
Pounding the rocks,
With its icy water,
Slowly eroding,
But unaware.

Then, further down the river,
The water is calm,
Peacefully winding down the hillside,
Until the next waterfall.

It's deafeningly peaceful,
From a distance it's a rainbow of light,
Colourful against the glowing sun.
Lower, to where it hits the river,
It is violent,
Pounding the rocks,
With its icy water,
Slowly eroding,
But unaware.

Then, further down the river,
The water is calm,
Peacefully winding down the hillside,
Until the next waterfall.

Ben J Gaunt (13)
Lady Manners School

LOVE?

Love an obsession, infatuation, idolisation.
Planted in your heart,
like a seed slowly growing and engulfing your soul.
Rotting your mind.
Stealing every second, every thought.
Is this true love?
Jealously and fixation
addiction, delusion.

Love, a passion burning within.
Wanting and longing the touch of their hand,
the flames of a desire hotter than hell
scorching your skin till you can take it no more.
Nights of bright white bliss
is this true love?
Just lust and passion,
pleasure, a thrill?

Love, a pain like a knife to the heart.
Like a window to the soul.
Cracking then shattering, the shards of
glass, cutting your skin.
Bleeding, hurting
a deep ache inside.
Is this true love?
Sorrow, depression.
blackness, death.

Briony Robinson (13)
Lady Manners School

I AM A ZOO

My mind is an owl,
It can weep or scowl,
Think of poems and rhymes,
And even fly away at times.

My hunger is an angry dragon,
When not fed it will madden,
Shouting, growling, pleading,
Until it is finally feeding.

My emotions are fish,
Swimming around as they wish,
Some are good, some are bad,
Some make me happy and some make me sad.

My life is a hare,
Rushing from here to there,
It will too soon be past,
And I will breathe my last.

I am a zoo,
And you are one too,
So are our teachers,
Made up of creatures.

Graeme Apthorpe (14)
Lady Manners School

VOLCANO

Like a roaring lion,
Hungry for blood,
Hurtles down the mountain,
Straight towards them.

They scream and run,
But no one can get away,
From the raging predator,
Who snaps at their heels.

In leaps and bounds,
It chases them,
Hot and fiery,
Determined to swallow all.

It slows,
And comes to a rest.
Mummified bodies,
Under its paws.

Rachel Gore (14)
Lady Manners School

THE INGREDIENTS OF A MAN

Their heads sugar doughnuts,
Jam for brains,
Their emotions are chocolate,
Melting when you open the packet,
Moving jelly for minds,
Hard to survive on one subject,
Marshmallows for ears,
Constricting them from every sound,
Their eyes minty polos,
Wide with desire, that dissolve with a blink,
Kinder eggs are their mouths,
Convincingly sweet outside that reveals a surprise,
Their hair strawberry bootlaces,
Hiding the truth of what's inside,
Men are like sponge cake,
So many ingredients inside to make up a sweet outside.

Holly Noyes (14)
Lady Manners School

GRAVEYARD

Graveyard
wet and windy
hear the owl up in the tree
wolf howling
footsteps coming closer
run
run
run!

Nicola Frost (13)
Parkside Community School

NATURE

The air is mild
The trees are wild
Sheep are grazing
The trees are rising.

Grass is growing
The river is flowing
Poppies are growing
The wind is blowing.

Simon Eyre (12)
Parkside Community School

GHOST

There are gravestones in the churchyard
And howling from the wolves.
There's an owl in the treetop
And a rattling from the door
And by the door
There's a spooky, scary miserable ghost
That stands there in a daze.

Lisa Bond (12)
Parkside Community School

GHOSTS

Ghosts are scary
Ghosts are spooky
Ghosts are white and creepy.
If you see a ghost tonight
You're bound to have a very big fright.

Andrew Howard (12)
Parkside Community School

WATER

I am water hot, cold, blue, clear.
You can find me in rivers, ponds,
streams, lakes and in the sea.
You can use me for washing and drinking.
A lot of animals live with me,
such as fish, frogs, dolphins, sharks,
whales, sea lions and starfish.
I can flood houses, towns, cities
and villages.
But I can come in useful for
putting fires out.

Laura Cooper (14)
Parkside Community School

BATS

Bats are black
they fly about
hanging upside down
at night
the moon shines bright
the bats wake up
open their wings
and catch their prey
ready to start
another day.

Sarah Cooke (12)
Parkside Community School

IN THE WOOD

Bats flying through the trees,
Rustling the leaves.
Monsters watching,
Evil eyes staring.
The moon is blocked by the treetops,
No light.
Gremlins brush through the bushes,
Sudden silence,
Blue-black sky,
No light,
Then,
Moonlight . . .

Clare Twigg (12)
Parkside Community School

GHOSTS ARE . . .

Ghosts are spooky,
Ghosts are scary,
Ghosts are tall,
Ghosts are airy,
Ghosts bring chills,
Ghosts bring shrieks,
Ghosts make clangs,
Ghosts make creaks.

Ghosts are *ghosts!*

Nicola Buxton (12)
Parkside Community School

SPIDER WEB

Silken silver threads
Reflecting ruby dew drops
A violet veil of velvet, shimmers
Dazzling raindrops like diamonds
Shadow of sapphire
Hem of purple threads
Knitted metallic braid
Sparkling strands of golden glitter
Glistening.

Rebecca Proctor (14)
Parkside Community School

THE WORM POEM

I saw
a little worm
one day, a-wriggling on its belly,
I looked at it for a little bit,
then squashed it with my welly.

Kelly Fox (12)
Parkside Community School

DOLPHINS

Splashing through green waters
like an arrow being thrown in the air
you leap from the depths
reaching to touch the sky
scattering spray
like rain on a summer's day.

Dawn Collyer (12)
Parkside Community School

ANIMALS' LOT

Now here's lot number 35,
A collection of things that once were alive.
An ashtray made from a gorilla's hand,
An elephant tusk umbrella stand,
A rhino horn, tiger skin rug,
An antelope head on a block of wood.
The price is going up in fives,
But that's not as much as the animals paid.
They paid with their lives.

Sean James Gormley (12)
Parkside Community School

THE ROLLER-COASTER

I step off the roller-coaster,
Everyone stares.
My face is all smudged,
And my hair's in the air.
It rises up high,
And swoops really low.
At the beginning it says,
Ready,
  Set,
    Go!

Kelly Laven (13)
Parkside Community School

REMEMBER

Remember the soldiers that went to war,
Who started a new life and walked through the door.
They fought in the fields where the poppies now grow,
They stand for blood and that's what they show.
They marched on blood-shod and lame
They didn't care although it was pain.
We pray for the families whose relations have died,
We know once families have cried
But now it's all over and people are dead
In everyone's eyes a tear is shed.
On the 11th month, the 11th hour and the 11th day
We remember the people who have passed away.

Jade Baker (14)
Parkside Community School

I AM AIR

I move, I rotate, I howl,
I fly like a swallow bird
I am wind
I can damage
I have power
I am oxygen, carbon dioxide and nitrogen
You can feel air on your face
You can hear air
And you can breathe me in.

Adam Burr (14)
Parkside Community School

I AM

I am the mountains with rough jagged rocks,
Clouds swirling round my cold, snowy tops,
I am the ocean seas with boats sailing, fish spinning and swimming,
                         ` dolphins jumping and diving.
I am the forest with dark-brown bark and bright green leaves.
I am the plants, the bright coloured petals, bringing bees to my lovely
                                    smelling pollens.
I am spinning, turning, floating, flooding.
I am Earth.

Kelly Walker (14)
Parkside Community School

BATS

The common flittermouse or bat
Lives inside a paper hat.
At night he flies about the sky
And makes an awful, creaky cry.

He paints his face with carpet glue
Because he likes to look at you,
And if your window he should pass
He'll stick his features to the glass.

Sophie Hooper (11)
Parkside Community School

SCHOOL

School,
People running to next lesson,
Can't be late,
Next lesson but the door is locked,
Oh no!
It's the extraction room for me,
I walk in there,
And I am the only one there,
Apart from the teacher,
It's a 4o minute detention,
Run to next lesson,
Forget my bag,
Run back,
Snatch my bag,
Just made it,
(Bell)
Yes, it's home time,
No more school for me.

Christopher Turner (11)
Parkside Community School

HAMSTER

H amsters are good fun,
A round the house they run.
M unching their food,
S ugar is my hamster's name.
T hey sleep in the day,
E very night they run on their wheels,
R olling around in their balls.

Claire Hill (11)
Parkside Community School

DOGS

Dogs are sweet
Dogs are playful
Dogs are strong
Dogs are everybody's favourite
Dogs are beautiful when they are puppies.

Dogs are very cuddly
Dogs are messy
Dogs are big
Dogs maybe violent
Dogs are forever.

Shauna Revill (12)
Parkside Community School

RED

Man U shirts are red,
So is my bed.
When the sun sets it's red,
So is the lit-up sky.
My blood is dark red,
My dragon top is red.
My striped socks are red and white,
Around my feet they are snug and tight.
My coat is black and red,
And so are poppies.
Eating apples are red,
Red is my favourite colour.

Elizabeth Proctor (11)
Parkside Community School

THE APPLE TREE

There was an old lady, her name was Daisy.
She had a little apple tree
and every time it shed its apples
she'd have a bag for me.
Some were red and some were green
but never a colour in between.
There were big ones and small ones
all juicy and ripe.
When I went back the very next day
I had a great surprise,
all the apples on the tree
had vanished before my eyes.

Gemma Blackburn (13)
Parkside Community School

HAMSTERS

Hamsters are small and fast
They run in a ball,
Around a room
And in their cage,
They run on a wheel.
They have sweet faces which look up at you
And whiskers that tickle,
When they explore.
Hamsters curl up when they go to sleep,
But disturb them and they will bite.

Natalie Timm (11)
Parkside Community School

COLOURS!

Blue is, the sky, the sea, the sign of coldness.

Red is, love, danger, a warning. *Stop.*
Red is the fiery afterbirth of hell.
Red is also Satan's blood.

Black is, gone, nothing.
Black is the night sky.
It's a bottomless pit.

Green is, the grass, the first leaves on a tree.
Green is the colour of an apple.

White is, fluffy clouds, the stars twinkling in the night sky.

Yellow is, the colour of the sun,
colour of a hatching chick,
a rubber duck in a bath.

Michael Taylor (13)
Parkside Community School

LIGHT AND DARK

The light is scared of the dark,
And the dark is jealous of the light!
The light holds energy,
The dark holds the winds!
But in the dark everybody fears the shadows!

Dean Watson (13)
Parkside Community School

A DIAMOND IS LIKE . . .

A room full of mirrors,
The eyes of a fly,
A sparkling bright star,
An ocean of sparkles,
Glitter spread across your eyes,
Raindrops sparkling on a leaf,
A marble rolling down the street,
The beads on your wedding dress,
Champagne sparkling in the glass,
The feeling of richness, you can see.

Laura Foyster (11)
Parkside Community School

THE SEA

The big dark blue waves
Crash against the rocks.
The pebbles rolling up and down the shore.
Wet sandy feet sink into the soft sand beneath the sea.
Crash, swish, round the rocks the sea flows,
Crabs scatter beneath the sea.
Jellyfish stinging people's feet,
Seagulls sitting on the rocks in the sea flying high and low.
Fish swimming away further through the dark blue sea.

Hayley Fox (11)
Parkside Community School

THE JUNGLE SALE!

When I went down to the jungle sale
I didn't think there'd be anything for me
Until I came across the animal stall
And there it was looking at me.

A big baboon with a head like a moon
All glowing like the sky
So I carried on walking
And still didn't know what to buy.

Then I came to the bric-a-brac
But I didn't want any of that.
I carried on walking free
Then I remembered that big baboon's for me.

I made my way to the animal stall
And made the greatest sale of all.

Sarah McNeice (14)
Parkside Community School

THE SEA

The big blue crashing waves
Crashing up to the sky
The seagulls flying higher and higher
The jellyfish sunbathing on the beach
The starfish swimming deeper and deeper
Pebbles sinking into the sand beneath the sea
The frozen footsteps washed away
It's the end of a wonderful day.
         The sea.

Emma Turner (11)
Parkside Community School

NEAR THE BEACH AND OFF THE BEACH

You hear the sea in between the caves.
You hear the waves crashing on the rocks
And you see the lighthouse shining the light across the sea.
You hear the boats hooting their horn,
You see the crabs in the rock pools crawling about
And when you try to pick them up
They try to run and hide and try to clip you.
When you are asleep all tucked up in bed,
You hear all kinds of things
Especially nature and it scares you half to death.

Cheryl Holtom (11)
Parkside Community School

THE SHADOW

The shadow, it follows me everywhere,
Even to bed, it's there when I turn on the light,
When I have a bath, it has a bath as well,
It doesn't talk,
It's as quiet as a mouse,
The shadow, it follows me everywhere,
Even on my bike,
And hides when the sun goes in,
I know that he's still there, because when the sun comes out
                                    he's back again,
I can't have any privacy anymore.

Chris Bunting (13)
Parkside Community School

WINTER!

Winter, ice, wind or snow, cold breeze and icicles are standing on
tiptoe.
Jack Frost is here once more, knocking at our front door.
'Yippee, yippee,' the children squeal, 'it's nearly Christmas Day.'
The children wrap up warm and snug and set off in the snow.
It's Christmas time once more, but remember it's not here for long.

Lauren Mellors (13)
Parkside Community School

THE SEA

The sea is like a swimming pool
A big bowl of soup
A never-ending river
A cold blanket of water
The biggest river you've ever seen.

Gemma Davison (11)
Parkside Community School

THE WIND

The wind rustles through the air, the sky.
The wind, cold, freezing, like the wind in winter.
The wind, warm and hot, like summer in July and August time.
The wind in December, cold, freezing, when the snow falls in January
and as it gets warmer, the wind begins to fade away.

Rachael Mapletoft (12)
Parkside Community School

THE STARS, THE MOON AND THE SUN

Stars
are like
dots gleaming in the sky.
A white ping pong ball floating
in the sky.

The sun
is like
the biggest fireball.
A big yellow cream egg.
A hot light bulb.
A big hot basketball.

The moon
is like
a big white banana
floating in the sky.

Christopher Findley (11)
Parkside Community School

SNOW

The snow is like . . .
a white blanket
lots of footballs falling from the sky
bits of candyfloss
loads of rabbits' tails
screwed up paper
bits of cloud.
The snow.

Marc Frobisher (11)
Parkside Community School

THE SEA

The sea so calm but underneath filled with anger
The sea like a rock climber climbing the cliffs
It is like a giant fish bowl with as many fish as you can imagine
It is like a hurricane swallowing boats
It is like a giant shark eating things alive
The sea is like a great big bath tub filled with people playing
The sea is fun for all
The sea is like a humungous fizzler as it crashes on the cliffs
Deadly, dangerous as can be
Washing up bottles, milk cartons, boots and pieces of boat
Underneath the waves the coral so beautiful
The sun goes in, the moon comes out, everything so still.

Arron Cocking (11)
Parkside Community School

BLUE IS . . .

A whale in the deep blue sea.
A Chesterfield top and their socks.
The nail varnish on my fingers.
The ink in my pen.
The paint on my wall.
The blueberries on the bush.
The pencil case on the table.
The felt tip in my pencil case.
The Smartie in the packet.

Samantha Swindon (13)
Parkside Community School

TRICK OR TREAT

T ricks in the dead of night.
R ight time of night.
I go to people's houses and give them a fright.
C urses and ghosts visit your house.
K nocks at the door to give you a fright at night.

O ut late at night.
R elease of demons.

T he dead of night.
R est in peace.
E verybody's out and about.
A mong the dead.
T ime to go to bed.

Carrieann White (12)
Parkside Community School

RED

Red is a car
Red is my pen
Red are my darts
And sticky jam tarts

Red is glory
Red is hate
Red is anger
Red is great

Red is England
Red is blood
Red is awesome
Red is good.

Andy Kelly (12)
Parkside Community School

I AM WATER

I am . . .

Wet, liquid, H_2O
Rivers, oceans, lakes
Blue, grey
Cold, clear
Neptune, Triton
Life, death
Salty, fresh
Fish, crab, dolphin, whale, turtle
Oasis
Waves, rain, cloud, stream, pond
Drinking water
Whirlpools
Ice, ice caps
Penguins
Green, seaweed
Disaster, Titanic
Power
Marine biology
Lifeboat, lifeguard, air sea rescue
Coastguard, Navy
Snow
Umbrella.

Chris Briggs (14)
Parkside Community School

CATS

Cats are soft
Cats are nice
Cats are always chasing mice

Cats are sleepy
Cats are fast
Cats are always running past

Cats are furry
Cats are cuddly
Cats are always in a muddly.

Michelle Harrison (11)
Parkside Community School

WATER

I am wet, cold. I am oceans,
seas, rivers, lakes, streams, ponds,
trickles, reservoirs and rain.
I am fish, whales, dolphins,
Neptune and Triton. I am snow,
hailstones, swimming pools and
condensation.

Haley Siddall (14)
Parkside Community School

THE MOON IS LIKE . . .

A great big plate.
A football.
A bird's eye view of a mushroom.
The sun, but dull.
The stars together without their twinkling light.
All different shapes.
The back of a metal spoon.
A large grey pebble.
A lump of concrete stuck in the sky.
The roads and pavement.
A piece of metal.
A cloud full of rain.
A grey or white balloon.

Laura McNeice (12)
Parkside Community School

CATS

Cats are fat
Cats are thin
Cats eat food from a tin
Cats get chased by dogs
Cats chase birds and mice.

Barbara McNeice (11)
Parkside Community School

THE MOTORBIKE RACE

'Mum, dad, there's a race today.'
'OK son, get down there to the bike, hurry up.
Open the garage first.'
'Dad, I am not silly.'
'Rev it up.'
'Bye Dad.'
'Bye son.'
In my head clicking sounds.
Crash! Bang! Bang!
Everything in pieces, even me.

Samantha Plater (13)
Parkside Community School

WITCH'S BREW

Double double toil and trouble,
Fire burn and cauldron bubble.

In the saucepan boil and bake
Put in a smelly rotten cake
Heart of a dog, ear of a pig
Liver of a human, depth of a dig
Foot of a newt, legs from a frog
Eye of a bird, leech from a bog

Double double toil and trouble
Fire burn and cauldron bubble.

Gareth Spolding (12)
Parkside Community School

TOIL AND TROUBLE

Double double toil and trouble
Fire burn and cauldron bubble
Skin of a worm and foot of a dog
Tail of a snake and toe of a hog
Two wings from a bat and one newt's head
Three cat's whiskers and a spider's web.
Double double toil and trouble
Fire burn and cauldron bubble.

Jennifer Motley (13)
Parkside Community School

UNDER THE GROUND

When I tunnelled under the ground,
I found under the ground,
Two wriggly worms,
Three manic moles,
Four scary spiders,
Five bothered badgers,
Six crazy cockroaches,
Seven biting beetles,
Eight clever centipedes,
Twelve wacky woodlice,
One sneaky snail snoring in his sleep,
And that's what I found when I tunnelled
under the ground.

Christina McKechnie (12)
St Thomas More School, Buxton

FREE

You dropped it on the floor,
The hard, dull shell smashed open,
The succulent, exotic juices burst out
And rolled away, they were free.

I imagined you in the same way,
Tough and dull on the outside,
But with me you opened up
Into a new person, you were free.

You swept me off my feet
With your love,
Your face and eyes were bright,
There was never a dull moment in your life.

But now, the brightness has disappeared,
My life is empty, and so is the coconut.

Sara Kamali (14)
St Thomas More School, Buxton

CONFESSIONS OF AN APPLE

Granny Smith always told us to be wary
  of the Braeburn.
Its sharp, sour taste was like biting
  into envy itself.

Its bright, deep, deep red skin,
  glistened, shone and lured you in.

But the Golden Delicious it must be said,
  was much more crunchy than the red.

Katie Shaw (14)
St Thomas More School, Buxton

HOLIDAY

The brown rough surface
Of the fruit
The rocks on the beach
Where we used to sit

The brightness of the yellow
Once you cut it open
The yellow shining sun
We stared at all day long

The pure fruit juice
Cold
The crystal clear swimming pool
We once swam in

The green spiky leaves at the top
Tall swaying palm trees
That kept us cool
In the hot burning sun

Once the fruit was cut
It was shaped in gold rings
Rubber rings we would sit in
When we relaxed in the pool

Now you have gone
And I am at home
Eating that pineapple
With all its lost memories.

Melanie Lath (14)
St Thomas More School, Buxton

GOODBYE FOREVER

My banana is my telephone,
I use it whenever I can.
I ring my friends to ask what's new,
And listen to their daily report.
I would keep it with me during schooltime too,
Didn't I tell you? It's a mobile.
But it gets rather squished in my rucksack,
That's the let-down with phones.
Its untidy splotches on its mustard skin,
Help me to dial secret locations.
I talk to people from unknown planets,
Exchanging knowledge and funny ideas.
It was all going smoothly until teatime today,
When I heard the most disturbing news.
I was just about to contact a friend in Fun World,
But I was stopped at a deadly halt.
'What's wrong with that banana?' I heard my parents say,
'Come on, chop chop, you haven't got all day.'
I tried to explain but they didn't understand,
And complained that I was becoming rude.
They don't approve of my adventures over the phone,
Or talking to a banana - they say.
So now I'm banned from bananas,
They're hoping I'll forget it that way.
But I'll never forget those people who had wonderful
                            conversations at tea,
I'll remember them forever and hope they remember me.

Kathryn McKechnie (14)
St Thomas More School, Buxton

WATERMELON WORLD

O watermelon,
with your firm, green exterior
you envelop your blazing core.
As I cut into your smooth protective skin
water seeps through
displaying a shimmering ocean of purity and health.
Your abundant wealth of seeds
are scattered on your ripe, pink surface,
like a miniature population.
You provide us
with the goodness we need to survive
by absorbing the sun's powerful rays of light and energy.
You are a micro image of our wonderful world.

Ruth King (14)
St Thomas More School, Buxton

REALISATION

You didn't realise how much you meant to me.
I trusted you and every time you said something hurtful,
I was bruised.
People said how colourful and bright I was,
But you peeled that from me,
Like the undressing of a banana.
You were stronger than I,
I couldn't cope with my skin black and brown with bruises.
I could no longer exist with the hurt I felt,
You had consumed my sweet insides and left my skin rotting.

Genevieve Moore (14)
St Thomas More School, Buxton

LEMON

Whatever happened?
The soft skin,
Exotic taste,
Untouched beauty
Bright, vibrant colours that used to be,
You changed
Now I see the real you.
Your colour turned dull,
That taste turned sour
Its fierce smell,
Bitterness that I would remember forever.
Until you faded
Shrivelled and disappeared
Our love was dead.

Catherine Hurst (14)
St Thomas More School, Buxton

YOU WERE ALWAYS THERE

You were always there,
Purple with passion and love
Your soft ripe skin
Smooth and silky against my cheek.

You were always there,
When I needed you. Plum.
Your flesh juicy, drips
Down my face in a stream of tears.

You were always there,
Until I came upon your inner core.
A side of you I'd never known.
Your side of hurt and betrayal.

You were always there,
Through good times and bad.
Then we shrank to nothing.
Shrivelled, no more than a memory.

Helen Barber (14)
St Thomas More School, Buxton

GEORGIA

Every time I see an apple, I see Georgia

The shiny red skin resembles her cheeks,
Smooth and ripe, like her youthful complexion.
I cut into the apple.
The white middle reminds me of her skin.
Juicy and ripe, she was once full of life.
I pick up the apple.
The dark brown pips are images of her eyes.
Shaped like her pupils, coloured like her long hair.
I see my neighbour outside.
Georgia was the apple of her father's eye,
She was all he had, since her mother's death.
I bit into the apple.
Looking back I hardly knew Georgia,
Though I saw her every day.

Every time I see an apple, I see Georgia.

Chantelle Salt (14)
St Thomas More School, Buxton

OUTCASTS

Like a child considered an outcast
the sprout sits on a plate ignored,
by the eater that hates it so.

Like a child considered an outcast
with the feeling of being unwanted
the small, greeny-white sphere sits,
waits, hoping to be taken, accepted as tasty.

Like a child considered an outcast
and thrown to one side,
the small tiny sprout lies on the plate.
It too has been parted from the other tasty dish,
the sprout may not be touched but neither will the fish.

Like the child considered an outcast
it's now the end of another day,
like a sprout being thrown into the bin
not staying on the plate where it once lay.

Matthew Scarbrough (15)
St Thomas More School, Buxton

DARK AND CHALKY

Dark and chalky,
Scratched and dented from the monstrous turns and tumbles,
Prehistoric layers of midnight show on its ancient skin,
Smooth like silk, yet as sharp as a dagger,
As black as burning charcoal,
Embedded in a mountain of dandelion-yellow sand.

Laura Martin (12)
St Thomas More School, Buxton

THE BALLAD OF STEPHEN LAWRENCE

Stephen Lawrence was a bright young lad
With plenty of good ideas
An ordinary black boy at the age of 18
Who didn't have many fears.

After a long day at college Stephen walked back
To the bus stop where he would stand
He was soon approached by 3 white youths
With something in their hands.

They called him names and pushed him down
Stephen was so afraid
They started to stab him with their knives
But could his life be saved?

When the police found Stephen's body
His parents were informed
So for months and months later
His family sat and mourned.

As the jury reached a verdict
Stephen's mother, Doreen, wept
And the killers they just laughed
As the Lawrences' lives were wrecked.

With smiles upon their faces
The three boys left the court
And seeing them set free
The Lawrences were distraught.

Five long years later
And the Lawrences still fight
For their son Stephen has been killed
Because he was black and *they* were white.

Caroline Wood (13)
St Thomas More School, Buxton

BEFORE I SLEEP

It's dark - it's still - heavy breathing -
my sister's fast asleep.
The clock's ticking - outside wind's blowing -
did I hear something creep?

Is there something in this room
that shouldn't be here at all?
Did something move under my bed!
What's climbing up the wall?

Curtains blowing -
Is something there? Go away!
But I can't speak -
my voice has gone - lost in the dark -
or - stolen by *night freak!*

I should've looked before the lights went out -
especially under my bed.
What's that - it's got my foot - be brave -
Oh! It's only Ted.

What's that noise -
it's faster - louder sounding.
It's getting closer - louder still
Oh! It's my heart pounding.

Be brave now Katie, go to sleep -
I'll close my eyes real tight.
There are no spooks or ghouls in my room -
I'm sure - I must be right.

Be brave now girl and say goodnight
to noises, shadows and sounds.
The dark won't hurt - it wants to sleep
with all that it
surrounds!

Katie Orridge (14)
St Thomas More School, Buxton

TO MY BEST FRIEND . . .

Never had a friend
strong and true,
Didn't know life
till I met you,
Words can't express
the way I feel,
I am living at last,
yet it doesn't seem real,
It was you who showed me,
that I was me,
banished my fears,
Set my soul free,
And it's you I'll speak of
when I'm old,
of secrets once shared
and stories once told.
I wrote this poem
to let you know
that you are my best friend
and I love you so.

Olivia Lawton (14)
St Thomas More School, Buxton

DUNBLANE

Another school morning,
In a little Scottish town,
How were mothers meant to know,
Their child would be shot down?

The screams of joy and happiness,
Turned into cries of pain,
In a few frenzied moments,
That morning in Dunblane.

A mad man named Hamilton,
With a killing desire,
Burst into their gym
And began to open fire.

He sprayed the hall with bullets,
As the children cowered in fright,
Little helpless children,
Could not put up a fight.

He killed sixteen lovely children,
And their teacher too,
He turned the gun then on himself,
And another bullet blew.

But for the parents of lost children,
Life will never be the same,
Nor for the village people,
In tragic Dunblane.

Jay Fisher (13)
St Thomas More School, Buxton

CHALLENGER

I'm going to tell you a story
Of a venture into space,
A disaster that was going to shock
The entire human race.

The members of the crew
Were the best of America's team,
They were going into space
To fulfil their country's dream.

The crew boarded the shuttle
It stood tall and proud
Looming over a watchful, but
Still excited crowd.

The countdown finally started
The booster rockets roared,
The shuttle lifted off the ground
Into the sky it soared.

The crowd were wild with excitement
As the shuttle climbed higher and higher,
Suddenly came gasps of horror
As it burst into a ball of fire.

Stunned into silence, were the crowd
Surrounded by a darkening sky,
As the fragments spiralled earthwards
All they could ask was, why?

Jennifer Thomson (13)
St Thomas More School, Buxton

CHERNOBYL ACCIDENT

It happened one day in '86
when technicians attempted a test
they were later to find they'd be in a fix
but they thought they were doing their best.

At 1.24 two explosions occurred
allowing the entry of air
a reactor fire resulted
which left the workers to stare.

The government tried to cover it up
and sprayed lots of water about
they evacuated the people
but eventually the Swedes found out.

The poison was carried by the wind
as far west as Wales and Spain
radiation contaminated sheep
by dropping in the rain.

Three years later the effects started to show
animals are born deformed,
an increase in cancer now occurs
and charities start to swarm.

Technicians are now thinking
of a way to repair the casing
still today the danger's not over
the concrete has started breaking!

Philip Hardman (13)
St Thomas More School, Buxton

ROSE

You arise from your bed, when the summer sun is shining down on you
A rosebud opening
I stand behind you and kiss your neck
I take a deep breath
You smell like a rose, so beautiful
I tell you what I think
Your cheeks turn rose with embarrassment
You plant a kiss on my lips so passionate
A rose scent remaining on my lips
You press your petal lips against my ear
'Ti adoro'

I didn't understand but it sounded romantic

You left for work, only a sweet scent remaining
You arrived back from work
You stood there upright and tall with pink rosy cheeks
You looked unwell
I gave you a cuddle, you prickled
Your scent had vanished
Your cheeks darkened
You wilted down to your bed
Rose petals falling to the ground

You might blossom again in the spring
You might never blossom again.

David Della Cioppa (14)
St Thomas More School, Buxton

PEACH KISSES

I feel its skin

Soft and smooth
Like when I touch your face
And run my fingers across your cheeks and lips

I take a bite

It's pure, heavenly and sweet,
Not unlike your tender peach kisses

I see its stone

It's strong, but safely wrapped in security,
That's how I feel when you hold me

I taste its flesh

It's as supple and velvety as your lips

And your tender peach kisses.

Vanessa Highet (14)
St Thomas More School, Buxton

THE PLAYGROUND

A desolate wilderness of concrete blankets,
Stretching out into awkward corners.
Litter wafts along the small gentle waves,
Spiralling seagulls attacking isolated rations.
Shouts, screams travel from St Anne's,
Children play full of life.
Keys jingle for the tuck shop door,
Being opened ready for break.

Shrills of bells releasing life,
Livening up tired students.
Chairs scrape along classroom floors,
People are ready to leave the classrooms.
An empty sheet becomes a space full of white shirts,
Flooded with footballs.
Girls gather in groups followed by boys,
Conversations begin in spots of a landscape.
The peacefulness is now eliminated by pedestrians.

Sergei Sellers (13)
St Thomas More School, Buxton

JACK

Like an apple with rosy-red cheeks,
Soft and tender, ready to eat.
Skin so smooth, clean and fresh,
Still and silent yet full of zest.

The shiny surface so appealing,
Bold and round with many colourings,
Marks and bruises distinguish you,
Sweet or sour and other things too.

Delicate, strong, beautiful and different,
Unique, sensitive and a soft white centre.
Weird and bright, outgoing and shy,
Jack, you are the apple of everyone's eye.

Bethan Youd (14)
St Thomas More School, Buxton

THE GOLDEN GLOBE

The future's bright in sunny Spain
Where glowing globes of light
Shine on through the night
And never fade away.

Their thick protective layer of skin
Keeps the tangy, juicy segments within
Untouched, safe from any harm
Like the sun beaming
High in the sky.

I peel that layer -
It is no longer needed
The closely-knit community
The countries of our shared world.

Not all the same
But connected in a special way
With the pith joining all the slices of the globe of light
And holding its sacred bonds very tight.

I eat a few of its special pieces
Suddenly it is no longer an orange
But a symbol of the
Sun's changing phases.

The orange is gone -
A reminder of my deep experience
My fingers marked by a sticky radiance.

Like the red-hot burning of my skin
The morning after a joyful swim
With the sun beating down
On my neck.

Fiona Edgar (14)
St Thomas More School, Buxton

THE WAY YOU ONCE WERE

The skin, bitter, sour and tough.
A clementine.
That's the way you once were.
Unpeel, slow and sure
So young, vibrant and sweet.
You changed.
Underneath that sour peel so coarse,
Is you.
The real you I miss.
After one clementine, I crave for more.
For you.
Not for the outer layer.
The way you once were,
But the way you are now,
The way you are now.

Ellie Butterworth (14)
St Thomas More School, Buxton

AS THE NIGHT WHISPERS

As the night whispers with dark velvet light,
As the moon glitters with white blazing light,
As the stars blaze with a great burning light,
You can hear the whispers of the dark cold old night.

As the night whispers with dark velvet light,
As the wind whooshes through trees, seas and fields,
As the rain pours down and birds flutter by,
You can hear the whispers of the dark cold old night.

Marie Dowd (12)
The Meadows Community School

BEING BULLIED

Being bullied, shoved around,
My life got turned upside down.
I got called this and I got called that,
My only friend was my auntie's cat.

I felt ashamed and all alone,
All I wanted to do was to go home.
The girls hated my clothes and the boys had a nose,
Why can't they leave me alone?

I started to cry, the girls didn't understand why,
I could feel them staring, glaring, chatting about me.
'Mardy mardy' is what they'd say,
I don't understand what I've done wrong.

I heard a voice and she called my name,
'Sarah, Sarah, Sarah-Jane.'
I looked around and she stood there,
Yes, someone who said she cared.

She told me to ignore them,
That's what I intend to do.
She told me we could be friends,
But that's not where it ends.

They all said I used her, they took her away,
But sure enough there she stood calling
My name 'Sarah, Sarah, Sarah-Jane
Come and stay with me till the end of the day.'

The girls call me names, but I'm not to blame,
I've got a friend who cares
And that's better than a million who don't.

Sarah-Jane Saint (14)
The Meadows Community School

SECRET

Tell me your secret
I promise not to tell
I'll guard it safely
At the bottom of a well.

Tell me your secret
Tell me, tell me please
I won't breathe a word
Even to the bees.

Tell me your secret
It will be a pebble in my mouth
Not even the sea
Can make me spit it out.

Daniel Morris (15)
The Meadows Community School

COMPASS

West the sun shines down on me,
East happiness comes for me,
South love comes for me,
North that's me the leader of the three
Oh please all of you be coming to me,
My friends are all of those.
But me I am the north the leader of the three,
So happiness, love and sunshine are all just for me.
If you put the three together it's called friendship,
Yes that's what's coming for me.

Nicole Highfield (12)
The Meadows Community School

THE LONG WALK

I went for a long walk one day
Grandad said he was going away.

He said I shouldn't be sad
even though I might feel bad.

'I'm happy that I'm going away
where I'm going I cannot say.'

Three days later Grandad died
I went back and knelt by his side.

I put some flowers on his grave
for my grandad I tried to be brave.

I had tears in my eyes
for here is where his body lies.

Adam Brear (12)
The Meadows Community School

A GOLDEN HEART

A golden heart stopped beating
Hardworking hands at rest
It broke our hearts to see you go
God only takes the best.
Your life was love and labour
Your love for your family true
You did your best for all of us
We will always remember you.

In tears I watched you sinking
I watched you fade away
And though my heart was breaking
I knew you couldn't stay.
Our lips cannot speak how we loved you
Our hearts cannot tell what to say
But God only knows how we miss you
In our home that's so lonely today.

Cherrelle Eyre (11)
The Meadows Community School

ME AND MY DAD

Me and my dad like scissors and glue,
I know I will never forget you,

Me and my dad like biscuits and tea,
Why did you have to leave me?

Me and my dad like the sun in the sky,
All I want to know is why.

Me and my dad like jam and honey,
Always there to lend me money.

Me and my dad like paper and pen,
I'd give anything to see you again.

Me and my dad like leaves on a tree,
Me and my dad, now it's just me.

Me and my dad, always together.
I wish you could be here for ever.

Clare Webley (14)
The Meadows Community School

SUMMER'S DAY

Once upon a summer's day,
In a wood far, far away,
Watching the birds in the trees,
A sunny day with a cool breeze.

Once upon a summer's day,
In a wood far, far away,
A cuckoo sings a sweet little song,
And didn't seem so very long.

Once upon a summer's day,
In a wood far, far away,
Watching the birds in the trees,
A sunny day with a cool breeze.

Jade Campbell (12)
The Meadows Community School

LIBRARY

Hot then cold,
I seem to be.
Hot then cold,
What can it be?
I look around then remember where I am.
I'm in the library,
And *bang* I hear the door slam.
So that's what it was all along,
The slamming of the door.
People coming in,
And people going out,
And here in the library nobody's supposed to
          Shout!

Lauren Royce-Dexter (13)
The Meadows Community School

MY HOLIDAY

My holiday to Skegness
Was a very big success
All the rides and all the fun
Then we got to have a bun
Lovely meal in the restaurant
Not much more could we really want
On the beach holes are dug
On the floor laid on the rug
Watching television my grandad sat
On the sofa with his hat
Fantasy Island is fantastic
Then my dad had to pull
On the rope at tug of war
And the rope nearly tore
Back at the caravan the ball hit the wicket
When we were having a game of cricket.

Vicki Moore (12)
The Meadows Community School

MY DAD

The day's so long, the night's so hard,
Without Dad by my side,
A tragic accident that took him away,
It's harder day by day,
I miss him so much but I'm trying to be strong,
Who'll be my friend when things go wrong?
He stood by my side in moments of need,
And cheered me along when I was trying to succeed,
He was the greatest dad in the universe,
Why did he go, was it a curse?
The funeral next week I try to forget,
It's all arranged, the day is set,
This is my chance to say goodbye,
I hope I don't break down and cry,
I loved my dad and he loved me too,
Just remember Dad, I'll never forget you.

Helen Oscroft (14)
The Meadows Community School

Now Dad's Dead

I'm feeling bad,
I'm feeling mad
As Longleat man
Has killed my dad,

He's ruined my life,
At night Mum cries,
Tommy wants to know
Why people die.

Lucy's upset,
But doesn't show it,
My dad's dead,
And Mr Longleat knows it.

He's got away,
No charge, no nothing.
But I know where he lives,
He's got a terrible thing coming.

I'm feeling bad,
I'm feeling sad,
I no longer have
My best friend, Dad!

Rebecca Slater (13)
The Meadows Community School

NOW DAD'S GONE

I don't know what to do now Dad has gone,
I feel really sad, but I don't want to tell,
I don't like crying in front of Mum,
because if I do she will start too.
I would love to see my dad again,
but how can I make him come back?
If only I could click my fingers,
then he would reappear.
Every night I look at the stars,
thinking that Dad is watching me.
Then when I'm in bed,
I think to myself,
if only I could catch that man,
and ask why he did it.
Why would someone kill my dad?
What did he do to them?
If only I could find out,
then it might make me a bit more happy.
When I go out I look around
and there are people staring at me
I think to myself
do they know what I'm going through?
If only they knew.
I would love to talk to them.

Katie Collins (13)
The Meadows Community School

REVENGE

He steps out of court
Thinking it's over
Not a chance
Nothing's over
He acts normal
He's no right
He's caused Mum grief
She cries at night
Even though Tom had to know
He still can't take it 'Dad had to go'
My sister just can't take it in
Now at night she's never in
Mr Longleat man just wait and see
Sweet revenge is up to me.

Rebecca Harvey (13)
The Meadows Community School

Autumn

Autumn is here after summer has gone,
the crackling of leaves under more feet than one.
Colours of rust like the sun's burning face,
leaves falling to the earthly ground with solemn grace.
Shapes and sizes of the covered earth,
each rising sun closer to winter's birth.
Breeze playing with the bronze branches of bloom,
swaying with the wind, waiting for winter's doom.
When spring shall arise and buds again will open,
small animals resting beneath the sheltering bracken.
Glowing cheeks to match the autumn's colour of glory,
shattered and empty trees until the death of winter's story.
Concluding and everlasting as the Earth goes on,
until one sad and mysterious day where everything shall be agone.

Sarah Bailey (13)
Tupton Hall School